*The*
# 5-Minute
# BIBLE
## Reading Plan
*and*
## Devotional Journal

BARBOUR BOOKS
An Imprint of Barbour Publishing, Inc.

This journal belongs to

...........................................................................

© 2018 by Barbour Publishing, Inc.

ISBN 978-1-64352-071-1

Written by Ed Strauss.

Scripture quotations marked KJV are taken from the King James Version of the Bible.

Scripture quotations marked NIV are taken from the HOLY BIBLE, NEW INTERNATIONAL VERSION®. NIV® Copyright© 1973, 1978, 1984, 2011 by Biblica, Inc.™ Used by permission. All rights reserved worldwide.

Published by Barbour Books, an imprint of Barbour Publishing, Inc., 1810 Barbour Drive, Uhrichsville, Ohio 44683, www.barbourbooks.com

*Our mission is to inspire the world with the life-changing message of the Bible.*

Member of the
Evangelical Christian
Publishers Association

Printed in China.

# CONTENTS

## Old Testament

## New Testament

# INTRODUCTION

Have you ever read the Bible from cover to cover? If you haven't, now is the perfect time to start. You may have been daunted by this task up till now. After all, the Bible is a big book. And you might have been tempted to think that it's mostly dull, dry history, unrelated to your life in the modern world.

God's Word is still relevant today, and it's well worth the effort to read it through, since it's wholly inspired by His Spirit. As such, it gives you an unparalleled look into the mind and heart of God. Even the sacrifices and rituals in Leviticus contain pertinent messages, as their fulfillment is found in Christ. And the recurring tales of disobedience in Judges and Kings are still relevant, since 1 Corinthians 10:11 states that these things happened to them as examples and were written for your benefit.

Don't put off reading the Bible a day longer. *The 5-Minute Bible Reading Plan and Devotional* breaks God's Word down into handy, bite-sized chunks, and you'll be able to read each devotional, together with the related portions of scripture, in just five minutes per sitting. You can either do your scripture reading daily or twice daily (morning and evening). However you do it, when you've completed this book, you'll also have read the entire Bible. And that's a major accomplishment!

# GENESIS

God existed before the physical universe (Genesis 1:1). He creates it and everything in it simply by speaking. The first two people, Adam and Eve, live in perfection but ruin paradise by disobeying God. Then the world's first child, Cain, murders his brother, Abel. People become so bad that God decides to flood the entire planet, saving only righteous Noah, his family, and an ark full of animals. Later, God chooses a man named Abraham as patriarch of a people called Israel after the new name of Abraham's grandson Jacob. Genesis ends with Jacob's son Joseph, ruling Egypt.

## GENESIS 1–2
### A Good Beginning

—————•❖•—————

God began a good work in His creation. The same powerful God who scattered the stars across the heavens, started the earth on its orbit, and breathed life into His creation, also began a good work by creating you. That doesn't mean that God expects you to be perfect. The Bible tells you that everyone sins (Romans 3:23), but it also says that sinners are redeemed through Jesus' sacrifice (v. 24). Today, celebrate the fact that God created you, set you on a course, and made a way for you to live forever with Him—all for His glory.

# GENESIS 3–5
## Redeeming the Fall

Evil entered the perfect world God created, and humanity fell into sin when Adam and Eve disobeyed and ate the forbidden fruit. As a result, all mankind died and the entire creation came under a curse and became corrupt. It may seem unfair that you were born into spiritual death and that all living things suffer for Adam and Eve's mistake. But God saved you, and one day He will completely renew you, giving you a powerful, glorious body that will live forever. And He will renew the whole earth, transforming it into a global paradise.

## GENESIS 6–7
### God in an Evil World

In Noah's day, all humanity was bent on doing evil. But fortunately, Noah, a righteous man, found favor with God, so He told him to build an ark to preserve his family and pairs of all animals. The world of Noah's day was similar to today's world. The earth was filled with crime and violence. Even though spiritual darkness covers the planet and you may wonder where God is at times, He's still caring and powerful. He hasn't forgotten you or abandoned you to the forces of evil. He's present to bless and watch over you.

## GENESIS 8–9

### Your Rainbow Promise

———•◦•———

After the Flood, Noah opened up the ark, and all the animals raced out and disappeared. Noah and his family were excited too, but before setting out to start new lives, they paused to sacrifice to the Lord. In return, God set His bow in the heavens, a promise that He'd never flood the earth again. Before hurrying out to your day's work, pause a few moments to seek the Lord. Give Him first place in your life. He may give you a promise too. Or He may reveal a solution to a vexing problem.

## GENESIS 10–12
### The Difference One Life Makes

God created every person on earth and loves them all, but in His wisdom and foreknowledge, He planned the life of one outstanding man. He had His hand on Abram (Abraham). Though Abraham made mistakes, his life was a hinge upon which the massive doors of history would turn. God gives you many promises today, and like Abraham you need to believe God. You too can profoundly impact the world and change history. Do you want to make a difference for God's kingdom? Then yield to Him. He can use you mightily.

## GENESIS 13–14
### Thinking of Others

Abraham gave Lot first choice of the land, and Lot, thinking only of himself, chose the lush Jordan Valley. But the well-watered plains attracted other greedy people too, and soon Abraham had to rescue Lot from the armies of five invading kings. Those who put themselves first often end up last (Matthew 20:16). You can bring trouble on yourself by pushing to the front of the line or by driving in life's fast lane and ignoring those lying wounded along the Jericho road. Think of others' needs as well, and God will bless you (Romans 12:10).

## GENESIS 15–17
### Waiting for God's Promise

———•◦•———

In Genesis 15, God promised Abraham that his own flesh-and-blood son would be his heir. In chapter 16, Abraham assumed Ishmael was that heir. But in chapter 17, God promised that a son named Isaac, born of Abraham's wife, Sarah, would be the one. God often makes promises to His people, promises that they sometimes try to fulfill by their own efforts. It's good to be proactive and to take definite steps—that's usually a necessary part of making dreams come true—but don't forget that this is, above all, God's work. Only He can bring it to pass.

## God the Just Judge

More than a few people think the destruction of Sodom and Gomorrah is a tale from God's wild and woolly days, before He reformed and became the God of love (1 John 4:8). But God is still the same. He declared that He is the Lord and doesn't change (Malachi 3:6). God still becomes angry at willful sin and disobedience and still avenges the oppressed when they suffer injustice. Read Revelation and you'll see how He plans to judge the world in the last days. That's a good reason for you to respect the Lord.

## Dealings with Philistines

---

Like Abraham, you may dwell in the midst of unbelieving "Philistines" and may be forced to have daily dealings with the ignorant and the ungodly. Abraham learned the hard way over an incident with Sarah that it's best to be up front and honest with people. Also, Abraham suffered in silence over a well that had been taken from him because he didn't want to bother the Philistine king. If you have a legitimate grievance, *tell* those in authority about it. Stand up. Insist on fair treatment. They may be unbelievers, but you still have rights.

## GENESIS 22–23
### The Lord Will Provide

---

When God Himself provided the lamb for Abraham to sacrifice in place of Isaac, this gave rise to a Hebrew proverb that His people's needs would be provided on the mountain of the Lord (Genesis 22:14). How does this apply to you? Well, when you're "on the mountain of the Lord"—whether involved in Christian ministry or faithfully obeying God in your daily life—He will see to it that your needs are met. As Jesus said, if you seek first the kingdom of God and His righteousness, all other things will be added to you (Matthew 6:33).

# GENESIS 24
## Romantic Tales

———————

When you think about it, it's rather amazing that this story—how God arranged the perfect wife for Isaac—has survived until today. Most of the surviving tablets and papyrus scraps from the rest of the ancient world are boring inventories of food and slaves and animal sacrifices. But God decided that this divine romance should be preserved for millennia in the scriptures. God cares for things that are important to you, your needs for love, romance, and physical intimacy. He hears your prayers for a companion. And He hears your prayers for a better marriage.

........................................................................................

........................................................................................

........................................................................................

........................................................................................

........................................................................................

........................................................................................

........................................................................................

........................................................................................

........................................................................................

........................................................................................

........................................................................................

## GENESIS 25–26
### Value Your Birthright

Esau sold his entire birthright for one bowl of lentils and a chunk of bread. The flocks and herds that he stood to inherit from his father Isaac were worth—in today's currency—tens of millions of dollars. He also traded away his rights to all the land of Canaan, some of the most expensive real estate on this planet. Thus, he became the very symbol of shortsighted, carnal, worldly people. Hebrews 12:16–17 warns against this. Be careful that you don't despise the treasures and riches of God's heavenly kingdom for a few temporary pleasures in this life.

## GENESIS 27
### The Stolen Blessing

Have you wondered why God allowed Jacob to deceive Isaac to receive his blessing then sanctioned his deception by allowing him to keep it? It was because Jacob already *had* the birthright. Isaac's blessing confirmed something that had already happened. But this is still a big lesson in trusting God. Are you ever tempted to make things happen by your own efforts? Are you sometimes willing to break God's laws to produce a desired outcome? Be careful, or you might run the train off the tracks in your eagerness to get what you want.

## God's Gate

---

When Jacob had a dream of God standing at the top of a wide flight of stairs, pronouncing blessings on him, he exclaimed that this spot was none other than the house of God, the very gate to heaven (Genesis 28:17). So he called it *Bethel* ("House of God"). Have you ever had an encounter with God, an experience that helped you realize His deep love and care for you? You probably haven't seen Him like Jacob did, but if He revealed Himself to you in any manner, treasure that experience. Let it give you strength.

## Contrary to Expectations

Jacob's uncle Laban agreed that only speckled, spotted, or streaked sheep would be Jacob's wages. Then he made sure that there were only sheep with white wool in Jacob's care. But *still* they kept bearing speckled, spotted, and streaked lambs. God did miracles to make their recessive genes come out. God still does miracles contrary to natural expectations today. He can make the least likely to succeed win. Is someone trying to defraud you? God can see to it that you're blessed despite their efforts to curse you or shortchange you. (See also 2 Samuel 16:11–12.)

## God Fights for You

When Jacob left Haran, he took his family and flocks and left without telling Laban. He knew he had to do that, or Laban would send him away empty-handed. Laban finally caught up to Jacob, but God had rebuked him the night before, telling him to watch what he said to his son-in-law. God is able to reprimand your adversaries as well. Don't think that your coming out on top depends on you having clever strategies, perfect arguments, or having lots of friends to back you. God is on your side, and He will fight for you.

........................................................................................

........................................................................................

........................................................................................

........................................................................................

........................................................................................

........................................................................................

........................................................................................

........................................................................................

........................................................................................

........................................................................................

........................................................................................

........................................................................................

## Wrestling with God

Jacob once wrestled with God—who appeared in human form—all night long. That was some exhausting match! Finally, God dislocated Jacob's hip so he couldn't wrestle anymore. But even that didn't stop Jacob. He simply clung to God and refused to let go until He blessed him. Christians today are sometimes said to "wrestle in prayer," but don't get the idea that you stand a chance of pinning the Almighty to the mat and forcing Him to give you what you want. Instead, simply throw your arms around Him and hang on to Him.

## Cleaning House

One day, Jacob found out that his wife, Rachel, had taken her father's idols (Genesis 31:30–34). Soon Jacob became aware that *many* of his herdsmen and servants secretly worshipped idols. So when great trouble struck and he desperately needed God's help, Jacob insisted that everyone ditch their gods (35:1–4). You cry out to God in your day of trouble, but often the first thing He does is to remind you of idols stashed in the corners of your life. They can be anything that competes with Him for your devotion, so clean house today.

## Prepared for Greatness

God had an astonishing plan for Joseph's life. God wanted to mightily exalt him, making him one of the most powerful men on this planet. But to accomplish that, God had to first test Joseph in the furnace of affliction—not only to see his motives but to humble him. God often does the same in your life by allowing you to suffer setbacks, calamities, and misunderstandings. You may wonder, "Why isn't God blessing me or protecting me?" He may be doing a special work in you, preparing you for service in His kingdom.

## Beware Alluring Voices

Joseph was the slave of a ranking Egyptian official named Potiphar, and as a young man, Joseph was well-built and handsome. This caused Potiphar's wanton wife to constantly entice him to come to bed with her. But Joseph knew that would ruin his life, so he steadfastly resisted. Is there someone speaking enticing words to you, trying to seduce you? Beware! They may be as alluring as the sirens of Greek myth, but they seek to bring you to ruin on destructive reefs (1 Timothy 1:19). Turn away from them, and don't yield.

## GENESIS 41
### Making Yourself Vulnerable

One night, Pharaoh had troubling dreams, and none of his wise men could interpret them. His cupbearer immediately thought of Joseph—but to mention him, the cupbearer had to bring up the subject of his *own* fall from favor two years earlier. He bravely chose to speak up. Has that ever happened in your life? To give context to a piece of information, have you had to talk about your own past mistakes? It's called making yourself vulnerable, and there's a measure of risk involved. But if you love others, you'll step up to the plate and do it.

## GENESIS 42
### God Sees and Hears

When Joseph's brothers came to Egypt to buy food, he recognized them but accused them of being spies. Not realizing who this "Egyptian lord" was, the ten brothers began speaking in Hebrew about how they had mistreated Joseph. Joseph, of course, understood them. God also hears your hidden thoughts and sees your secret deeds. The Lord's eyes are in every place, keeping watch on the evil and the good (Proverbs 15:3). So watch what you say and think! Be prayerful about what you do. You'll one day have to give an account to Him.

## GENESIS 43–44
### Deeply Buried Love

---

After Jacob was led to believe that Joseph was dead, Judah was so disturbed by his father's grieving that he moved away from home (Genesis 37:31–35; 38:1). Now, to spare his father new pain, Judah offered to become Joseph's slave—proving he truly loved his father (44:16–34). Past strife may have also led you to put space between you and your family. But may love—often deeply buried love—move you to do the right thing in due time, reconcile with your loved ones, and let go of old offenses and forgive.

## GENESIS 45–46
### Moved to Tears

One of the most emotional parts of the Bible is when Joseph broke down and wept, revealing to his family that he was their long-lost brother. You may sometimes complain, like Jacob, that your life has been painful and difficult (Genesis 47:9), but may you experience a happy ending that moves you to tears. Like Joseph, you may have endured abuse and bullying at the hands of family members, but know this: God desires times of sincere forgiveness and reconciliation as well. It may cost you to take the first step, but it's so worth it.

# GENESIS 47–48
## Stay on Your Knees

---

Joseph respected the prophetic anointing his father had, so when he brought his two sons to Jacob to be blessed, he bowed down (Genesis 48:12). But when Jacob placed his right hand on the younger son's head, Joseph arose and took his father's hand to move it (v. 17). Are you sometimes like that? Do you tell God you desire to yield to His will and obey Him, yet when what He does displeases you, you attempt to move God's hands and make Him do things *your* way? It's best to stay on your knees.

———•◆•———

Why did God promise that the ruler's scepter would not depart from Judah (Genesis 49:10) when Reuben was Jacob's firstborn? Why were Israel's kings from Judah? Well, Reuben sinned grievously (35:22), so he was out of the running. Levi and Simeon disqualified themselves by a bloody massacre (34:25). So Judah, the fourth-oldest, was chosen. God has plans for you too, but if you fail or refuse to fulfill your mission, He will look for someone else who will obey. Are *you* willing to stay obedient to God so He can use you?

# EXODUS

After Joseph dies, a new pharaoh sees the Hebrews as a threat and makes them his slaves. God speaks to Moses through a burning bush and sends him to demand the Israelites' release from Egypt. To break Pharaoh's will, God sends ten plagues on Egypt. Pharaoh finally allows the Israelites to leave and God parts the Red Sea for them. At Mount Sinai, God gives Moses the Ten Commandments and His Law, but the people worship a golden calf, bringing judgment on themselves. Exodus ends with the people continuing their journey to the promised land of Canaan.

## EXODUS 1-2
### It's Not All about You

———•◦•———

The Lord told Abraham that his descendants would be slaves in another land, but that after four hundred years, they'd be delivered (Genesis 15:13–14). When Prince Moses came along, he concluded that he was that deliverer. He assumed his fellow Israelites would realize God had sent him (Acts 7:23–25). When God has given you outstanding talents and gifts, you too may feel assured that He has a mighty calling on your life. He may well have. But remember, to succeed you must depend on God's strength and wisdom not your own charisma and abilities.

## EXODUS 3–4
### He Feels Your Pain

———•◦•———

God was aware of the suffering of the Hebrews and told Moses that He knew their sorrows (Exodus 3:7). The Lord knows every bit of your suffering too, and sees every tear you shed. Jesus was called a man of sorrows, acquainted with grief (Isaiah 53:3). He knows when you experience sorrow, and He feels your pain. In all His people's suffering, He also suffers (63:9). You may cry out, wondering why God doesn't act immediately. But wait on Him. In His time, He will act. In the meantime, He's right beside you.

## EXODUS 5–6
### No More Straw

————— ·◦· —————

When ordered to let the Israelites go, Pharaoh made their lives even more miserable. From that day on, the Egyptians didn't supply the straw they needed to make bricks. The Israelites had hoped for imminent deliverance; instead, their bondage increased. You may be implementing new time-saving methods at work only to find the steep learning curve makes your job even harder. Or you may be praying for better finances only to be hit with another bill. Have patience. Give God time and space to work. He will eventually bring good results (see Hebrews 10:36).

## Plagues upon Egypt

Despite God sending one nationwide plague after another on Egypt, Pharaoh stubbornly refused to let the Israelites go. But God knew he'd react this way. In fact, God had counted on it, as this gave Him opportunities to prove that He alone was God, that He had power over nature, and that the gods of Egypt were powerless before Him. Even today, you can get a sense of awe of the Almighty during a thunderstorm, while watching a glorious sunset spread across the sky, or in exploring the wonders of His creation in a nature video.

## EXODUS 9–10
### Natural but Supernatural

———•◦•———

Scholars note that the first nine plagues of Egypt were events that naturally occurred there from late summer to spring. For example, hailstorms happened in January/February. The difference? God warned that He would send the *worst* hailstorm that had *ever* fallen on Egypt (Exodus 9:18). God often uses natural events today, amplifying them in a miraculous way to bring about His will. If you're paying attention, you'll see God at work. But you might sometimes wonder if it was really a miracle. Rest assured that God's fingerprints are on even the "natural" things of life.

## EXODUS 11–12
### The Meaning of Passover

The Feast of Passover began when the Hebrews living in Egypt smeared the blood of a lamb on their doorposts. When God saw the blood, He *passed over* the house, sparing the firstborn within. But He slew all the firstborn Egyptians. The New Testament tells us that Jesus is the ultimate Passover lamb, and He shed His blood so you might live (1 Corinthians 5:7). When John the Baptist saw Jesus, he told his disciples to behold the Lamb of God who takes away the sin of the world (John 1:29). Are you glad that *your* sins are forgiven?

## Crossing the Sea

When you read the Psalms, you'll notice how often the parting of the sea is mentioned. The Israelites referred to it as the greatest miracle in their nation's history. It was *the* defining event of the exodus, a miracle that set the founding of the Hebrew nation apart from all others. But did it literally happen? Yes, it did! The God who created a billion swirling galaxies, with gargantuan star-devouring black holes at the core of each, has no trouble making water solid for a few hours. He does it at the North Pole all the time.

## Bread from Heaven

---

The Israelites found themselves in the Sinai Desert without food. So they complained. But the next morning when the dew evaporated, something that looked like frost was left behind. It was manna, a miraculous wonder bread, and God continued to supply it for forty years. In John 6:32–35, Jesus compared Himself to manna, saying that He was the bread that came down from heaven. Do you take time every morning to seek His hidden manna and have your spirit refreshed? Have you eaten the Bread of Life and absorbed Him into your very being?

## EXODUS 17–18
### Listening to Advice

———•◦•———

Moses' father-in-law, Jethro, the priest of Midian, came out to meet him in the desert. Then Jethro saw Moses judging disputes between Israelites. There were long lineups of people waiting to speak with Moses, so Jethro told him that he needed to let others help him judge. It's good to have a wise, older friend you can go to for advice—someone who's lived a long life and has learned a few things along the way. Do you have someone like that? Moses was a prophet yet he humbled himself to receive fatherly advice, and you must too.

## EXODUS 19–20
### The Ten Commandments

————◦————

One of the first things that happened when the Israelites reached Mount Sinai was that God gave them the Ten Commandments. It was a top priority on God's to-do list, and people have been pondering these commands ever since God inscribed them in stone. But He really yearns to write His law on your heart. That way you'll always be aware of them and be inclined to obey them. And if you love the Lord and love your fellow man (Deuteronomy 6:5; Leviticus 19:18), you'll be sure to obey all ten commands.

## EXODUS 21–22
### A New Legal Code

People sometimes wonder why there are so many laws in the Old Testament, but remember, Israel was a brand-new nation and needed laws to govern them. Today we have many more laws than the Israelites had. In fact, in addition to national and state laws, every city has bylaws. You'll find it easy to obey all these laws if you love your fellow man. In fact, you'll probably obey the law—both God's and man's—without thinking. Laws exist to protect people's rights, and if you're careful not to violate others' rights, you'll get along just fine.

## EXODUS 23–24; EXODUS 25:1–9
### Helping Your Enemy

What would you do if you saw an enemy trip and drop an armload of groceries? You might be tempted to laugh, then keep right on walking, thinking, "It did me good to see that!" But even in the eye-for-an-eye days of the Law of Moses, God forbade this attitude. According to Exodus 23:5, you are to help your enemy. So Jesus wasn't saying anything shocking and new when He commanded you to love your enemies (Matthew 5:44). It was embedded in God's law from the beginning. But you must choose to see it.

## EXODUS 25:10–40; EXODUS 26
### Articles for Worship

———•◦•———

When Moses was on Mount Sinai, the Lord showed him what to make—
the ark of the covenant, a golden table, a lampstand (a menorah), an
incense altar, and the tabernacle to house these articles. You may
wonder why God wanted the things used in His worship to be made
of gold. This is to show their great value. And Hebrews tells us that
these items were a mere shadow of heavenly things (Hebrews 8:5). The
*heavenly* temple, altar of incense, and ark of the covenant (Revelation
8:3; 11:19) are made of far more priceless materials.

........................................................................................................

........................................................................................................

........................................................................................................

........................................................................................................

........................................................................................................

........................................................................................................

........................................................................................................

........................................................................................................

........................................................................................................

........................................................................................................

## Here I Come

---

People who go hiking in grizzly bear country are advised to attach small bells to their backpacks, boots, or walking sticks. Bears may attack when surprised, but if they can hear you coming, they won't be startled by you. There was a similar idea behind the high priest wearing small golden bells on the hem of his garment (Exodus 28:33–35). Now, the priest couldn't startle God, but the bells showed respect for Him and kept the priest from being slain. God is utterly holy, and people are not to presumptuously enter His presence—even now.

.......................................................................................

.......................................................................................

.......................................................................................

.......................................................................................

.......................................................................................

.......................................................................................

.......................................................................................

.......................................................................................

.......................................................................................

# EXODUS 29
## Dwelling among You

Why did God tell the Israelites to wash Aaron and his sons with water then dab the blood of a ram on their bodies? God desired to live among the Israelites (Exodus 29:45–46), but their sin was an offense to Him. He couldn't live and move among His people until their sin was taken away. Jesus' blood cleanses you today, but you must confess your sins and repent of them to be forgiven (1 John 1:7–9). God calls you to holy living, so you must deal with sin before His Spirit can be present in all His fullness.

## EXODUS 30–31
### A Trademarked Scent

God instructed the Israelites to make a special anointing oil of select ingredients. He said to make these into a sacred anointing oil, a fragrant blend, the work of a perfumer (Exodus 30:25). This fragrant oil was for anointing the high priests and holy objects, so people weren't to produce it for their private use. Jesus is our high priest (Hebrews 4:14), and in Song of Songs 1:3 the Bride of Christ says that the fragrance of His perfume is pleasing, and His name is like perfume poured out. Treat Jesus and His name with the respect they deserve.

## EXODUS 32–33
### Do-It-Yourself Religion

While Moses was on Mount Sinai getting commands on how to—and how *not* to—worship God, the Israelites made an idol of a golden calf. That was their idea of God. Aaron then declared a festival to the Lord, so what did the people do? They threw a wild party. They got everything wrong. People today do similar things. Blithely ignoring the Bible's declaration that forgiveness is found only in Jesus, and cobbling together their own religion, which states that all religions are valid paths to heaven. Take the time to ponder what God says.

## The Beauty of God

---

When Moses came down from Mount Sinai after spending forty days alone with God, he wasn't aware that his face was radiant from being with the Lord. But the people could see the light of God on his face (Exodus 34:29–35). Your entire life is changed when you're in the habit of daily spending time seeking God, praising Him, and meditating on His Word (see Psalm 34:5). If you contemplate the Lord's glory, you're transformed into His image with ever-increasing glory (2 Corinthians 3:18). Spend time with God today.

## God-Given Talents

It was time to make the tabernacle and all its articles, and the Lord told Moses that two artisans, Bezalel and Oholiab, were to lead the craftsmen in this work. They knew how to do everything from cutting gems to goldsmithing to weaving. Like Bezalel and Oholiab, there are multitalented people today who amaze you with the songs they write, the movies they produce, and innovative methods in getting out the Gospel. But even the way you care for others is beautiful. And remember, it's God who inspires you and gives you your abilities.

## EXODUS 38; EXODUS 39:1–31
### Gems and Eternal Souls

————◆◆————

When Bezalel and Oholiab made the high priest's breastpiece, they mounted twelve gems on it—one for each tribe of Israel (Exodus 39:10–14). These included jewels such as turquoise, lapis lazuli, emerald, agate, and topaz. These precious stones represented Israelites of the various tribes. Like the Israelites, you are far more valuable to the Lord than any earthly gemstone because you're an eternal, living creation of God with an amazing destiny. Zechariah 9:16 says that the Lord will save His people and that you will sparkle like jewels in a crown.

## The Cloud of Glory

Moses often entered God's presence. In addition, he spent a total of eighty days with God on the mountain. But when he dedicated the newly built tabernacle, even Moses couldn't enter the tent of meeting because the cloud, the glory of the Lord, so filled it (Exodus 40:35). You're now able to enter the presence of God in prayer, to come before His throne, but don't ever treat the Lord lightly or casually. He's a holy, all-powerful God. And since you are now His dwelling place, the temple of His Spirit, be careful not to defile yourself (1 Corinthians 3:17).

# LEVITICUS

❦

Leviticus, meaning "about the Levites," describes how the family line of Levi would lead the Israelites in worship. The book provides ceremonial laws as opposed to the moral laws of Exodus, describing offerings to God, dietary restrictions, and purification rites. Special holy days—including the Sabbath, Passover, and the Day of Atonement (Yom Kippur)—are commanded. The family of Aaron, Moses' brother, is ordained as Israel's formal priesthood. Leviticus lists several blessings for obedience and many more punishments for disobedience. The New Testament books of Romans, Galatians, and Hebrews give Leviticus a Christian context.

## LEVITICUS 1–3
### Sacrificial Offerings

———◆———

Leviticus provides great detail about the proper way to make sin offerings, burnt offerings, and fellowship offerings. People in the ancient Near East were familiar with such sacrifices. Abel, Noah, and Abraham sacrificed lambs. So did the pagans of Ebla, centuries before Abraham. The difference was, Leviticus taught people how to do it God's way—and its sacrifices were to the true God not to pagan idols. Jesus is the ultimate Lamb, sacrificed for you. His death on the cross for your sin is the ultimate fulfillment of the sacrificial lambs of Leviticus.

## Sinning Unintentionally

These two chapters describe how to make a sin offering or a trespass offering. But these offerings only covered your sin if you sinned unintentionally. What if you *knew* what you were doing, like so many people today? And what if you committed adultery or murder? There was no forgiveness for those sins. You were to be executed. But through Jesus you *can* be forgiven for all your trespasses. Through Him everyone who believes is set free from *every* sin, a justification you were not able to obtain under the Law of Moses (Acts 13:39).

## Making Things Right

The Israelites were counted unfaithful to the *Lord* if they deceived their neighbor, swore falsely about him, kept something he'd lost, or cheated him. (This explains Psalm 51:4.) They were to make things right by confessing to their neighbor, making restitution in full (*plus* some), and then sacrificing a ram to God (Leviticus 6:1–7). These days, you must first confess your sins to God then confess to the person you've wronged. You're also to be willing and ready to make restitution to them. God cares deeply about people's rights. When you hurt them, God Himself feels their pain.

## The Priests' Portions

———•◦•———

Priests in Israel had a demanding job. They were constantly being splattered with blood as they butchered oxen, sheep, and goats. But there were benefits. God allotted choice portions of meat to them (Leviticus 7:31–34). Most Israelites rarely ate meat, but priests enjoyed it frequently. What undesirable tasks do you have? Now think of the benefits of faithfully and diligently carrying out those tasks—not the least of which is having steady, paying work. Your work may be taxing or tedious, but do it diligently and faithfully, and God will bless you for it.

........................................................................................

........................................................................................

........................................................................................

........................................................................................

........................................................................................

........................................................................................

........................................................................................

........................................................................................

........................................................................................

........................................................................................

## LEVITICUS 9–10
### Disrespecting God

————◆————

It may seem harsh that fire came out from God's presence and killed Aaron's sons, Nadab and Abihu. But their disrespect was quite serious. Apparently, when the brothers offered incense before the Lord, they had sauntered directly into the holy of holies (Leviticus 16:1–2). Even the New Testament says to serve God acceptably with reverence and godly fear, for He is a consuming fire (Hebrews 12:28–29). You wouldn't carelessly shove a fork into an electrical socket, after being warned not to, then complain about getting shocked, would you?

Leviticus 11:6 says that the rabbit chews its cud, but Bible critics insist that's wrong—they don't. However, they do. Rabbits excrete *cecotropes*—cuds of half-digested plants. These are rich in vitamin B12, which rabbits need, so once they're excreted, they're immediately re-eaten. Modern critics are constantly disparaging the Word of God for so-called errors or contradictions, but you can confidently read the scriptures, knowing that they are true. However, not all doubters are simply trying to find fault. Some people have sincere questions, and if you can answer them, they're more open to the faith.

## Skin Diseases

---

From the descriptions given—and their rapid changes—it's clear that these skin diseases weren't leprosy. There were lepers in Israel too, and Jesus healed them, but there were several other infectious skin diseases in Bible times. In Exodus 9:8–11, God sent festering boils on the Egyptians—probably skin anthrax. But He promised those who love Him that He's the Lord who heals, so He wouldn't bring any diseases upon them which He'd brought upon the Egyptians (Exodus 15:26). If you *get* a skin infection, chances are good God isn't judging you. He didn't send it.

## LEVITICUS 13:47–14:32
### Mold and Mildew

———•◦•———

God gave the Israelites regulations concerning mold. If you get mold or mildew in your home, don't think God sent it to punish you. (So feel free to spray it with disinfectant.) The fact is, mold spores are in the air all around you. You can take it for granted, for example, that all bread will become moldy if left out long enough (Joshua 9:5). That's why Jesus said to store your treasures in heaven, where moths won't eat your clothes, where oxygen won't rust your valuables (Matthew 6:19), and where mold won't fill your walls.

## Washing and Quarantines

---

The Bible was thousands of years ahead of medical discoveries when it commanded people with a running sore or a discharge to wash themselves, their clothes, and their bedding, and to be quarantined. God gave practical instructions on cleanliness to Moses about 1,450 BC. But modern doctors didn't wash their hands before examining patients or performing operations until 1846, when Dr. Ignaz Semmelweis instituted it in his hospital. As a result the death rate from infectious diseases dropped dramatically. This goes to show that God knows what He's talking about, so you do well to listen to His instructions.

## LEVITICUS 16–17
### The Day of Atonement

———•◦•———

Once a year, the high priest was to sacrifice a young bull as a sin offering for his sins and the sins of his household. He was then to enter the holy of holies to sprinkle blood on the ark of the covenant. Then he was to sacrifice a goat for the Israelites' sins. The New Testament says that Jesus is your high priest and that He entered the Most Holy Place in heaven itself. He purchased eternal redemption for you by His own blood (Hebrews 9:12, 23–25). Praise Him for loving you that much.

## LEVITICUS 18–19
### Love Your Neighbor

————◆————

Many Christians have difficulty reading through Leviticus with its chapters of now-obsolete ceremonial cleansings, repetitive details on blood sacrifices, and less-than-thrilling descriptions of mold spreading on walls. But one of the two most vital commandments in the Bible, hidden in these dusty pages, says that you are to love your neighbor as yourself (Leviticus 19:18). Many Bible books may seem dead and dry at first glance, but they contain truths that can breathe life into your being. Jesus says that the words He speaks to you are full of the Spirit and life (John 6:63).

## LEVITICUS 20–21
### Mediums and Spirit Guides

In ancient Israel, people who acted as mediums or who consulted the spirits of the dead were to be put to death because they defiled God's people (Leviticus 20:27; 19:31). They defiled people because they received their power from evil sources. There's no longer a death penalty for being a medium, just as there is none for committing adultery, but you should still avoid mediums just as you avoid adultery. Seek the Lord instead. He has promised that if you do, He will show you great and amazing things that you knew nothing about (Jeremiah 33:3).

## LEVITICUS 22; LEVITICUS 23:1–22
### A Sacrifice without Defect

When God commanded the Israelites to offer sacrificial animals to Him, He specified that they must be without defects—in other words, without warts, sores, injuries, or other blemishes. The apostle Peter informs you that Jesus is just such a sacrifice, a lamb without blemish or defect (1 Peter 1:19). Jesus lived His whole life without sin, thus He was the perfect sacrifice, chosen by His Father to take your punishment upon Himself. Spend time meditating on how much Jesus loved you, making Him willing to suffer so terribly to save you.

## Hebrew Holidays

In the previous reading, and in this one, Moses describes six great festivals that the Israelites were to celebrate annually. The Day of Atonement was a somber event, as was Passover, but most Jewish festivals were joyous celebrations and contained specified days of rest. God is concerned about His people's health and well-being. He not only commands you to rest one day a week but desires you to enjoy rest and recreation throughout the year. Don't drive yourself too hard, or you'll burn out. Enjoy yourself and spend time with your family.

## The Land Belongs to God

God solemnly promised the land of Canaan to Abraham's descendants. But as with any contract, it pays to read the fine print. God also declared that the land belonged to Him. The Israelites were only foreigners and temporary tenant farmers working for Him (Leviticus 25:23). Like the Israelites, you too are just a short-lived day laborer on this earth. You may amass possessions and own land, but in the end, you must leave it all behind. You brought nothing into this world, and it is certain you can carry nothing out (1 Timothy 6:7).

## Dedicating Things to God

Sometimes Israelites dedicated people, land, or livestock to the Lord. People still did this in Jesus' day, but the problem was that they sometimes gave land or money—and received recognition and praise for their generosity—when they should have used those things to support their aged parents (Mark 7:10–12). It's good to give generously to your church, but be sure that you're taking care of your family's needs as well. You may enjoy being praised for giving, but you have a duty to care for your family (1 Timothy 5:8).

# NUMBERS

Numbers begins and ends with a census—hence the book's name. After the Israelites escape Egypt, they number 603,550 men (Numbers 1:46), not including Levites. They head to the Promised Land, but complain about food and water, rebel against Moses, and hesitate to enter Canaan because of the powerful people living there. God therefore decrees that the entire unbelieving generation will die in the wilderness, leaving the Promised Land to a new generation of obedient Israelites. At the end of the forty years, they take a second census, and the total number of Israelite men is only 601,730 (26:51).

# NUMBERS 1
## Know Your Resources

The Israelites were about to invade Canaan, so God told Moses to do a census to get an accurate idea of how many fighting men they had. Knowing their troop strength would help the Israelites plan their campaigns (see Proverbs 24:6; Luke 14:31–32). Whenever you're planning a building project or any project, it's wise to know the resources you have available—including manpower, material, and finances. If you're to counsel with others about an endeavor, you need to be aware of the facts in order to hold a meaningful discussion.

## Getting Organized

God instructed the twelve tribes of Israel to pitch their tents in distinct, separate areas of camp, around their tribal standards. This kept them organized. Also, when it was time to travel to a new place, it enabled them to set out in a particular order. These may seem like uninspiring practical details, but it pays to organize your work area and your daily schedule. That way, you prevent confusion and frustration, avoid wasting time, and can find things easily. Also it ensures that you'll have time for daily Bible reading and prayer.

## NUMBERS 3:14–4:16
### Making the Way Open

——————

The Levites weren't numbered among the men of military age because they took care of the tabernacle, dismantling it, moving it, and setting it up. Each Levite clan had responsibilities, so they camped right around the tabernacle. However, only the high priests could enter the inner sanctuary (Numbers 3:38; Hebrews 9:6–7). These days, *all* believers may enter God's inner sanctuary. You have direct access into the presence of your Father. Jesus made the way open and cleansed you completely from your sins by dying for you (Hebrews 10:19–22). What a tremendous privilege you have!

## Even for a Moment

---◆---

As mentioned in Numbers 3:27–31, the Kohathite clan's duty was to carry the holy articles of the tabernacle. But first Aaron and his sons covered them with cloths. The Kohathites weren't allowed to touch them or even to glance at them, lest they die. Do you treat the things of God with great respect? If God gives you a ministry, do you understand clearly what a privilege it is, do you follow its rules faithfully, and are you aware that it's only by His grace that you serve Him in this capacity?

## Nazarites

---

The tribe of Levi was set apart for God's service, especially dedicated to Him. But *all* Israel was a "nation of priests" (Exodus 19:6), so Israelites from all tribes sometimes wanted to dedicate themselves to the Lord and spend time apart from daily activities, drawing close to Him. So God arranged for them to temporarily become Nazarites (Numbers 6:1–21). You too may feel God calling you to draw aside to spend time in fasting and prayer, seeking the Lord or engaging in short-term missions, etc. Respond to His call.

## NUMBERS 7:1–71
### Matching Donations

———◆———

This chapter describes the Israelites' offerings at the dedication of the tabernacle, and for many people, it's a boring chapter. Moses describes all twelve tribes, one by one, giving the *exact same* sacrificial animals and donations. You may wonder, "Why repeat it twelve times?" But focus on the main message: *everyone* should give to God's work. Besides, it doesn't hurt to be reminded of things. Peter wrote that he wouldn't be negligent to remind believers of the basic truths of the faith, even though they already know them and are established in them (2 Peter 1:12).

## Out-of-Season Passover

God commanded the Israelites to celebrate the Passover at a specific time, once a year, or be excluded from their nation. But God knew that people sometimes had legitimate reasons why they couldn't participate—so He made exceptions (Numbers 9:1–14). The Law could be severe when people flagrantly disobeyed it, but its heart was love. Jesus summed up God's attitude when He quoted His Father saying that He desired mercy and not sacrifice (Matthew 9:13; Hosea 6:6). It's the same today. You are still to obey God, but not legalistically. Jesus stresses love and forgiveness.

## Led by a Fiery Cloud

For forty years, the cloud of the Lord's presence hovered over the tabernacle as a cloud by day and as fire by night (Numbers 9:15–23). The only time it moved was when the children of Israel were to travel to a new location. God's presence is no longer marked by a pillar of cloud and fire, but you can still be sure that He's with you. In fact, He has promised to never leave or forsake you (Hebrews 13:5). Be sure you follow God wherever He leads. He's in you, yes, but you must also walk within His footsteps.

## God Miraculously Provides

---

Where could Moses find enough meat to feed the multitudes of Israelites in the desert? It would have taken a miracle. And that's exactly what God did—a miracle! You might think that He doesn't do amazing things today, that it's just up to you to provide for yourself. Well, you *must* work to earn a living, but it's God who gives you the strength and the wisdom to work (see Deuteronomy 8:17–18). And you can still count on Him to help you and do truly outstanding wonders to provide for your needs when you can't help yourself.

## Don't Fear Giants

---

What especially unnerved the ten fearful spies in Canaan was the sight of the towering, ponderous Anakim, nine feet tall and massively muscled. The Israelites were certain they couldn't conquer them. There was even a proverb: "Who can stand before the Anakim?" (Deuteronomy 9:2). Even today, many people have an innate fear of tall people or large creatures. What giants do you fear? What problems cause *you* to become anxious? Trust in God. He can strengthen you in dire situations and help you overcome larger-than-life difficulties. They might be bigger than you, but God is much bigger than them.

NUMBERS 14:26–45; NUMBERS 15

## Just What You Ask For

———•◦•———

The older generation of Israelites didn't have faith that God could help them conquer Canaan, so they moaned that it would be better if they simply died in the desert. Therefore, God gave them exactly what they had the faith for: they all died in the desert. God has many good things planned for your life, but you'll never receive them if you don't believe that He is willing and able to provide them for you. According to your faith will it be done unto you—so believe God wants to bless you! (Matthew 9:29; see also Isaiah 7:9).

.................................................................................................

.................................................................................................

.................................................................................................

.................................................................................................

.................................................................................................

.................................................................................................

.................................................................................................

.................................................................................................

.................................................................................................

.................................................................................................

.................................................................................................

### Aaron's Staff Bears Fruit

God sometimes chooses unlikely people to accomplish His will, to lead a ministry, or to do amazing things. You might be painfully aware of that person's faults and all-too-human failures and question whether they're worthy of that position. One day, the Israelites questioned Aaron's leadership. After all, hadn't Aaron made an idol of a golden calf? But when Moses asked God to reveal whom He favored, God caused Aaron's staff to bud and bear fruit. When you want to know if God is in someone's life, look at the fruit they bear (Matthew 7:20).

## NUMBERS 18–19
### Tithes to the Levites

The Israelites were commanded to give God one-tenth of their income, and the Lord then stated that He was giving all these tithes to the Levites for the work they did serving at the tabernacle (Numbers 18:21). This principle is still valid. Paul explained that in New Testament times the people who preach the Gospel should be supported by it (1 Corinthians 9:14; see also 1 Corinthians 9:1–11). Whether you believe in tithing or not, as a New Testament Christian, you should give faithfully to support your church, your pastors, and your church's workers and missionaries.

.............................................................................................................

.............................................................................................................

.............................................................................................................

.............................................................................................................

.............................................................................................................

.............................................................................................................

.............................................................................................................

.............................................................................................................

.............................................................................................................

## NUMBERS 20–21
### Water from the Rock

Forty years earlier, God had provided water for the Israelites when Moses struck a rock with his staff (Exodus 17:1–6). This time God told him that if he'd just *speak* to a rock water would flow out. But Moses angrily whacked the rock. You might find yourself in a situation that riles you, but restrain yourself. If you act in anger or proceed in your own strength, you may make a bad situation worse or even create new problems. If God tells you to speak gently, do so, and trust Him to do a miracle (see Proverbs 15:1).

## NUMBERS 22; NUMBERS 23:1–12
### Balaam's Donkey

---

You know Balaam was pretty far off track when God had to use his *donkey* to get through to him. He was rebuked for his disobedience by a pack animal, a beast normally without speech, who rebuked him for his greed (Numbers 22:28–30; 2 Peter 2:15–16). Even today God's children sometimes ignore His voice, refuse to obey His Word, and shut their ears to godly counsel, until the only way God can get their attention is to do something unusual—and often painful. Listen to His rebukes and He won't be forced to chasten you (Revelation 3:19).

..............................................................................................

..............................................................................................

..............................................................................................

..............................................................................................

..............................................................................................

..............................................................................................

..............................................................................................

..............................................................................................

..............................................................................................

..............................................................................................

..............................................................................................

## NUMBERS 23:13–30; NUMBERS 24–25
### Obeying God in All Things

———•◦•———

When Balaam feared God, he was used mightily, even giving a prophecy about the King of Israel. He declared that a star would come out of Jacob and a ruler's scepter would rise out of Israel (Numbers 24:17). This was fulfilled when a wondrous star shone at Jesus' birth. Yet Balaam soon fell into such grave sin that the Israelites killed him (Numbers 31:8). There's a powerful lesson here. It's not enough to have served God in the past or to be obedient in *some* things. Continue to fear God today and obey Him in all your ways.

# NUMBERS 26
## A Net Loss

When the Israelites left Egypt, Moses took a census. There were 603,550 men (Numbers 1:46). In a census forty years later, there were only 601,730 men (26:51). Why 1,820 *less*? Because the Israelites had worshipped Baal, so God sent a plague killing 24,000 men (25:9). You may wonder why you've worked for decades but have little to show for it. You might be living month to month and may have even been forced to declare bankruptcy. Why is this? Perhaps you ignored God's financial principles. But sometimes too, life is just plain hard (Ecclesiastes 9:11).

## Commissioning Joshua

Moses learned that he'd die before the Israelites entered the Promised Land, so he asked God to appoint someone in his place. God chose Joshua (Numbers 27:12–23), Moses' right-hand man and a proven leader. You too should know who will replace you when you can't finish things. This applies whether you're leaving a job, departing from a ministry, or vacating some position of responsibility. Make sure that the person taking over your position is qualified and has a heart for the work. Also make sure they have the keys, the files, and the necessary authority.

## Objecting to Rash Promises

God told Moses that if a man heard his daughter make a rash vow, he was to nullify (invalidate) it on the spot (Numbers 30:1–16). To remain silent was to consent to it. At times, you'll overhear one of your children giving away all their toys or money and will need to step in and put on the brakes. Or you may hear your wife—or for women, your husband—make an overly generous offer and will need to say, "Actually, we need to discuss this first." In all cases, it's vital that you speak up at once.

# NUMBERS 31
## When Friends Become Foes

Moses' wife was a Midianite, and his father-in-law was a priest of God, so Midianites were once godly, but things had changed over the decades. They now worshipped Baal, and their women led many Israelite men into idolatry. So God told Moses to do battle with Midian. Similar dynamics exist in families when some members become Christians and others oppose Christ (Matthew 10:34–36). This is also true of former friends. Sometimes they slander you because you're no longer partying and drinking (1 Peter 4:3–4). Never mind what they do. You follow God.

## Jumping to Conclusions

The tribes of Gad and Reuben saw that the land east of the Jordan was good grazing land, and since they had many cattle, they asked Moses if they could settle there. Moses thought they were refusing to help the other tribes conquer Canaan, so he became upset. But that wasn't the case. How often do you jump to conclusions as well and misjudge others' motives? James advises you to be swift to hear, slow to speak, slow to wrath (James 1:19). So avoid making accusations. Instead, ask questions and hear people out. You'll be glad you did.

## Boundaries of Canaan

---

Numbers 34 describes the borders of Canaan. The Israelites occupied most of this land with one major exception: their heritage extended *far* to the north, as distant as the Euphrates (Deuteronomy 1:7). But the farthest the Israelites under Joshua occupied was a few miles north of the Sea of Galilee. Like the ancient Israelites, many believers today don't live up to their full potential. They're satisfied with little prayer, almost no Bible reading, and scant giving. As a result, they fail to occupy the complete heritage God intended for them and only fulfill part of their destiny.

## NUMBERS 35–36
### Hatred and Murder

———————

God stated that murder polluted the land and said that His people must not defile the land where they lived, for He lived there Himself (Numbers 35:33–34). Here's how this principle applies to your life: 1 John 3:15 says that anyone who hates another person is a murderer. That's why Jesus commanded you to love your neighbors and even to love your enemies (Matthew 5:44; 22:39). Hatred in your heart pollutes it, and it grieves God's Spirit to live in a heart harboring hatred. This is why Jesus tells you repeatedly to love others.

# DEUTERONOMY

With a name meaning "second law," Deuteronomy records Moses' final words as the Israelites prepare to enter the Promised Land. The entire older generation has died, so as the new generation prepares to enter Canaan, Moses reminds them of God's commands and their national history. The invading armies will be led by Joshua, as Moses will only get to see the Promised Land from Mount Nebo. Then Moses, the mighty prophet of God, dies, and God buries him in a valley in the land of Moab. Moses had lived to be 120 years old.

# DEUTERONOMY 1; DEUTERONOMY 2:1–7

## Sacred Spaces

The Israelites camped beneath the shadow of Mount Sinai for two years. There God met with them, gave them the Law, and had them build the tabernacle to worship Him. Finally, God told them that they had stayed long enough at that mountain. They were to break camp and leave (Deuteronomy 1:6–7). God daily calls you to meet with Him in the sacred place under His feathers, close to His heart (Psalm 91:1–2, 4). There your spirit is renewed. Then, confident that God is with you, you can venture forth to face the day.

..................................................................................................

..................................................................................................

..................................................................................................

..................................................................................................

..................................................................................................

..................................................................................................

..................................................................................................

..................................................................................................

..................................................................................................

## Others Conquered Giants

The Israelites feared giants called Anakim. But God pointed out that the Moabites had conquered the giant Emim, the Ammonites had vanquished the gigantic Zamzummim, and Cretans had wiped out the monstrous Avvim (Deuteronomy 2:9–11, 19–21, 23). Likewise, you need to believe that *you* can defeat giants. You're not the first to face huge obstacles. Believe that, God helping you, you can overcome them too. They may loom large in the road ahead, but God gives you power and authority over them. Don't be fearful. Advance boldly and expect victory.

# DEUTERONOMY 4
## God Is Near

—•◦•—

Moses asked what other nation was so great as to have their gods near them the way the Lord their God was near the Israelites when they prayed to Him (Deuteronomy 4:7). It's encouraging to know that God is near you when you seek Him. He has promised to dwell in the midst of His people. In fact, since Jesus sent forth the Holy Spirit, He dwells within your heart (Galatians 4:6). Because Jesus' blood purifies you and gives you access to God's presence, you can boldly come before His throne and pray for whatever you need.

## DEUTERONOMY 5–6
### Love God Passionately

———— • • ————

Moses quoted the Ten Commandments a second time, and after enjoining the people to obey them, declared that they were to love the Lord their God with all their heart, with all their soul, and with all their strength (Deuteronomy 6:5). Jesus later said that this was the greatest commandment, and all heartfelt obedience flows out of it. You may find, however, that it's difficult to keep focused on it. Too often, you'll default to meticulously obeying lesser commands, merely modifying your outward behavior to please God. But don't miss out on the heart of the matter.

## DEUTERONOMY 7–8
### Breaking Down Altars

———•◦•———

God told the Israelites that, after they had conquered Canaan, they were to destroy the altars of the pagan gods, break their sacred pillars, cut down their wooden images, and burn their carved images (Deuteronomy 7:5). How does this apply to you today? What altars and images do you need to tear down? You're most likely not tempted to worship Baal or Asherah, but are you giving in to greed and materialism? Paul said that they too are idolatry (Colossians 3:5). Or are you captivated by society's images of beauty and happiness? Tear those images down.

## DEUTERONOMY 9–10
### Realistic Self-Assessments

When God lets you accomplish something, it's easy to get the impression that you're pretty hot stuff. You may secretly think that the reason God gave you success was because you're better than others—or more deserving. Beware such attitudes. God cautioned the Israelites that after they'd conquered Canaan, not to think that the Lord had brought them there to possess the land because of their righteousness (Deuteronomy 9:4). Actually, it was only because the Canaanites were so wicked. Paul also cautions you not to think you're better than you really are (Romans 12:3).

## Blessings on Your Life

---·•·---

God influenced the weather to bless His people when they, as a nation, corporately obeyed Him. He told the Israelites that Canaan was a land He cared for, and His eyes continually watched over it from the beginning of the year to its end (Deuteronomy 11:12–14). Even if your nation is disobedient and God can't bless them corporately, if you personally obey God faithfully and consistently, you can expect Him to send blessings on *your* life in due season (Genesis 39:2–5). Maybe not exactly when you want them, but in their season.

...........................................................................................

...........................................................................................

...........................................................................................

...........................................................................................

...........................................................................................

...........................................................................................

...........................................................................................

...........................................................................................

...........................................................................................

...........................................................................................

...........................................................................................

## Exploring Other Religions

---

Since time immemorial, youth who have been brought up in Christian homes have been intrigued by other religions. The forbidden has a strong enticement. They're sometimes drawn away into mysticism and the occult, Buddhism and witchcraft. One thing that especially appeals to them is that many other religions leave their adherents free to live selfishly or promiscuously. God knew this would be a problem with later generations of Israelites (see Deuteronomy 12:29–31), since Baal worship, for example, was very lascivious. This is why God commanded His people to completely eradicate pagan altars and idols.

# DEUTERONOMY 15–16
## Cancelling Debts

———•———

Besides the Old Testament command to tithe, God commanded His people to faithfully practice other financial principles. For example, at the end of every seventh year, they were to cancel the debts of every Israelite who owed them money (Deuteronomy 15:1–3, 7–10). You may not always be in a position to practice this, but the principle behind it still applies. Paul said that you are to do good to all people, especially to fellow believers (Galatians 6:10). Jesus went further, commanding you to lend to your enemies without expecting to be repaid (Luke 6:35).

## DEUTERONOMY 17–18
### The King's Scroll

In Israel, the king was commanded to keep a copy of Moses' Law with him and to read from it daily. That way he would be aware of its requirements and obey them. And it would prevent him from becoming proud and acting as if he were above others (Deuteronomy 17:18–20). For these same reasons, you today should have a personal Bible and read it daily. Many mistakes and sins come about simply because believers haven't read their Bibles and don't know what it says to do (Matthew 22:29).

## DEUTERONOMY 19–20
### False Witnesses

In ancient Israel, warnings against being a false witness usually referred to not giving an untrue testimony in a court of law (see Deuteronomy 19:15–21), where lying statements could cost someone their life or a hefty fine. But you need to guard against telling untruths in smaller, everyday matters also. When you damage or lose someone's belongings, do you shade the truth just enough to keep out of trouble? When recalling a conversation, do you leave out details that would make you look bad? Speak the *whole* truth and nothing but the truth.

## Returning Lost Property

———— ⧫ ————

A modern proverb says, "Losers, weepers. Finders, keepers." This is *not* scriptural. The Bible says that if you see someone's ox, sheep, or donkey wandering, you are to return it to him—or hold it and wait for him to come looking for it. This same rule applies if you find his clothing or wallet or any other possession (Deuteronomy 22:1–3). God stipulates that you're not to ignore it. Don't just walk on by thinking it's too much hassle to try to reunite something with its owner. You're to get involved and take responsibility for it.

———◆———

Deuteronomy 24:6, 10–11 contain practical, compassionate laws safeguarding the rights of the poor. Lenders couldn't take his tools as security because that's how he earned a living. And they couldn't just barge into his home to seize his belongings like some modern debt collectors do. Jesus also stressed being considerate of the needs and the rights of the poor. It's a big part of how you show your love for God. For example, if you've lended money to a friend or family member, be considerate of their financial situation before insisting that they repay immediately.

........................................................................................

........................................................................................

........................................................................................

........................................................................................

........................................................................................

........................................................................................

........................................................................................

........................................................................................

........................................................................................

## Honesty in Business

---

In ancient Israel, one of the most virulent scams was having two differing weights—one heavy, one light—to overcharge customers. People also had differing measures—one large, one small (see Deuteronomy 25:13–15). Dishonesty and defrauding others are still rampant today, whether price gouging or hidden fees. Greed, coupled with a lack of love for one's fellow man, fuels all corrupt businesses. But Christians are to be known for their love and honesty. Paul wrote that love does no harm to a neighbor, thus love fulfills the law (Romans 13:10).

## Blessings for Obedience

Some believers spend a great deal of time praying for God to bless them. But they forget the other half of the equation—they must *obey God*. The Bible promises that if you consistently love God and obey Him, many blessings will follow you and overtake you (Deuteronomy 28:2). You'll scarcely need to seek them. You'll be relentlessly pursued by God's blessings. You won't be able to escape. They will chase you, catch up to you, and overwhelm your life. Then you'll always be at the top not at the bottom (v. 13).

## Curses on Disobedience

---

God warned that if His covenant people consistently disobeyed Him, He'd send escalating waves of punishment until every area of their lives was affected. This passage gives a withering list of curses, but some people ignored them, smugly assuming they'd be safe even if they persisted in their own way (Deuteronomy 29:19). But remember, God punishes sin. As a Christian, you're not subject to God's wrath; however, in His love He will chasten and discipline you to bring you back into line if you disobey (Revelation 3:19). So stay close to Him and be obedient.

---

Even though God threatened to judge Israel in anger, He wouldn't forsake them. He promised that though He had scattered them to distant lands, if they repented, He'd tenderly gather them and care for them once again (Deuteronomy 30:1–6). This is surely true of His children today also. You may have turned from God and deeply backslidden, but His love for you never falters. This depth of compassion surprises many people. They think that once God is upset with them, it's all over. But God is never finished with His people. He loves you eternally.

# DEUTERONOMY 32
## God's Care for You

Many people, when they think of the Israelites in the desert, think of complaining, disobedient, stubborn people being judged repeatedly by an angry God. That was the older generation. But in reference to their children, God describes Himself as shielding them and caring for them in a howling, barren land. He describes Himself as a mother eagle hovering protectively over her young, carrying them aloft in a picture of miraculous grace, and spreading His wings to catch them when they fall (see Deuteronomy 32:10–11). This is a perfect picture of God's relationship with you as well.

## DEUTERONOMY 33–34
### Carried on God's Shoulders

In Deuteronomy 33, Moses pronounced blessings on the twelve tribes, and you can appropriate these for your own life. One blessing was that the beloved of the Lord would rest secure in Him, shielded by Him all day long, resting upon His shoulders (Deuteronomy 33:12). Jesus described a shepherd seeking lost sheep and joyfully carrying them home on his shoulders (Luke 15:4–6). When you gave your heart to Him, you became the beloved of the Lord, so rest secure in Him. He shields you all day long (see 2 Thessalonians 3:3).

# JOSHUA

God now tells Joshua to lead the people into Canaan.
In Jericho, the prostitute Rahab helps the Israelite
spies and earns protection when the city is destroyed.
God knocks its walls flat as Joshua's army marches
around it, blowing trumpets and shouting. Joshua
leads several successful military campaigns to drive
out the Canaanites, and God even answers Joshua's
prayer to make the day last longer so they can finish
a battle (10:1–15). Major cities subdued, Joshua
divides the land among the tribes of Israel, reminding
the people to forsake their idols and to passionately
seek the Lord their God (24:23).

## JOSHUA 1–2; JOSHUA 3:1–6
### Prosperity and Success

You may wish to memorize Joshua 1:8 and quote it to remind yourself that if you continually meditate on God's Word and constantly refer to it during the course of your day, He has promised to make you both prosperous and successful. This doesn't just refer to material prosperity, but to God's blessings in all areas of your life. And verse 9 urges you to be strong and courageous, to not give in to fear or discouragement, because the Lord your God will be with you wherever you go. Pause to meditate on these promises today.

## JOSHUA 3:7–17; JOSHUA 4–5
### *Drying Up the Jordan*

---

God performed a miracle by making the Jordan River stop flowing. Bible scholars tell us that God probably caused the cliffs to collapse into the narrow gorge thirty miles upstream, damming the river. It stopped flowing the exact instant the Israelites stepped into the water. Has God done any miracles of precise timing in *your* life? Has desperately needed money arrived just in time? Has someone you urgently needed to speak to suddenly contacted you? God is still in the business of doing miracles—often through natural events and ordinary circumstances.

## Jericho's Walls Fall

From 1930–1936, an archaeologist named John Garstrang dug at the ancient city of Jericho. The Bible says that the wall fell down flat (Joshua 6:20), and Garstrang found that Jericho's walls had indeed collapsed–falling outward, away from the city. You can rest assured that the Bible is God's inspired Word, the actual history of real events, accurate down to its tiniest details. God had this Bible account written for your benefit, to encourage you, inspire you, and move you to love Him more. Put your trust in the Lord.

## JOSHUA 7:16–26; JOSHUA 8
### Pausing to Pray

——•◦•——

After conquering Jericho and Ai, Joshua led the Israelites to Mounts Gerizim and Ebal to read the Law and renew their covenant with Him. Had you been in Joshua's place, after winning those initial battles, you might have felt like striking again while the iron was hot, but Joshua had his priorities straight. God had told him to go there (Deuteronomy 11:29–30), so he went at the first opportunity. Spend time with God. You may be victorious now, but it's wise to pause and pray, and spend time meditating on His Word, lest you stumble.

## The Power of Prayer

In Joshua 9, so-called ambassadors from a distant country came to the Israelites, wanting a peace treaty. Joshua didn't pray and ask God for wisdom, so he made a big mistake (9:14–15). But when he *did* pray in the next chapter, God did an outstanding miracle (10:12–14). Think of your own life. Can you ask God for wisdom when making decisions and expect Him to give it to you? Most certainly! (See James 1:5–6.) Can you ask God to do a mighty miracle to help you finish a job? If you have the faith, yes (Mark 11:24).

## Victories and Mopping Up

Joshua defeated a large alliance of southern armies in a single battle then rapidly took one city after another. He quickly followed by crushing a colossal coalition of armies in the north. Then came years of mopping-up campaigns (Joshua 11:18). That's often the way life is: you experience major breakthroughs in bursts of inspiration followed by long periods of slow, steady–almost boring–plodding. You may wonder, "Why can't my *entire* life be a series of thrilling victories?" Sorry. You must learn to be satisfied with the glory days God gives you (see Ecclesiastes 7:10).

## Becoming Responsible

After five years of war (Joshua 14:7, 10), Joshua, like Caleb, was about eighty-five. God told Joshua that he was now very old, but there were still very large areas of land to be taken over (Joshua 13:1). But now it was up to each tribe to conquer the Canaanites in their area. This parallels your life. When you were young, your parents cared for you, but when you came of age, you took responsibility for your own support and decisions. It may have been a tough transition—maybe still is—but it was necessary and worth it.

## JOSHUA 14–15
### Fighting for a Cause

———•◦•———

Caleb was eighty-five, an age when most people had been retired for twenty years already. But he was still strong enough for battle. Some forty-five years earlier, God had promised to give him Hebron, a city of giants, and he was now eager to take it. How about you? If you're retired, are you content to spend your days watching TV and engaging in leisure activities, or do you still desire to march forth for a great cause? If you're younger, don't give up your dreams when you're battered by life. Hang in there!

........................................................................................................................................................................

........................................................................................................................................................................

........................................................................................................................................................................

........................................................................................................................................................................

........................................................................................................................................................................

........................................................................................................................................................................

........................................................................................................................................................................

........................................................................................................................................................................

........................................................................................................................................................................

........................................................................................................................................................................

........................................................................................................................................................................

## JOSHUA 16–18
### Who Is More Determined?

————•◦•————

Joshua 17:12 says that the Israelites tried to drive out the heathen, but that the Canaanites were determined to dwell in that land. The Israelites wanted them out, but the Canaanites were intent that they weren't going anywhere. Many obstacles and habits in your life are like that. Your mind may be set on stopping smoking, but your body is determined to continue getting nicotine. You may want to stop having negative or lustful thoughts, but they keep popping into your mind. What can you do? Like Joshua, you must often wage war a long time (11:18).

## Everyone's Fair Share

When Joshua retired, he divided the land of Canaan between the twelve tribes. The more populous tribes received larger portions of land, and the less numerous ones received smaller portions. Everyone got their fair share. You may often face situations where you must fairly apportion resources and give equally of your time. It begins with chocolate bars and works its way up to a family inheritance. Pray for God to give you wisdom. Some people may still feel unfairly treated, but if you've done your best to be fair, that's all God expects.

## Towns for the Levites

———•◦•———

The Levites didn't receive their own territory, but each tribe gave them some cities to live in. When they cast lots in Judah, the city of Hebron went to the Levites. God had promised Hebron to Caleb, so how could God give it away? Well, Caleb kept the surrounding villages and fields (Joshua 21:9–12). Like him, you may have fought hard to make your dreams come true only to see someone else share in their revenue. It may not seem fair, but God is good. It helps you to realize that others have needs as well.

## Suffering for Doing Good

After the war, when soldiers from the tribes of Gad, Reuben, and Manasseh were crossing the Jordan River to go home, they stopped and built an altar. This well-meaning, innocent act nearly caused a war. You may know how that feels. You also might have attempted to do good and been misunderstood. It's bad enough to be called on the rug for your faults. But it's demoralizing to suffer unfairly. However, the apostle Peter promised that God will reward you if you patiently endure undeserved suffering (1 Peter 2:20).

## JOSHUA 23:11–16; JOSHUA 24
### It Costs to Serve God

When Joshua told the Israelites to choose which god they would serve, they answered that they wanted to serve the Lord. But Joshua replied that they weren't able to serve Him because He was a holy, jealous God who wouldn't just overlook their rebellion and their sins (Joshua 24:19). Now, however, you *can* serve God because He has forgiven your sins through Jesus Christ. He is still a holy God. He still becomes jealous when your heart turns from Him to other things, so be zealous and repent (Revelation 3:19).

# JUDGES

After Joshua's death, the Israelites lose momentum and many tribes don't drive out the pagans in their midst—with tragic results. God warns His people that since they didn't obey Him, the remaining Canaanites will lead them into idolatry (2:2–3). That's exactly what happens, and the Israelites begin a cycle of worshipping idols, suffering punishment by attackers, crying to God for help, and receiving God's aid in the form of a human judge (deliverer) who restores freedom. Lesser-known judges include Othniel, Ehud, Tola, Jair, and Jephthah, while more familiar figures are Deborah, Gideon, and Samson.

## JUDGES 1–2
### Finishing the Job

---

After Joshua's death, the men of Judah went to war and conquered the remaining enemy strongholds. But most Israelite tribes were unable or unwilling to drive out the Canaanites in their territories and allowed them to continue dwelling with them. Well begun is half-done, but it's *not* a finished job. What unfinished conquests are on your doorstep? You may have started to clean house spiritually, but are there still stubborn strongholds of the enemy in certain areas? You shouldn't expect to conquer them all at once, but you do have to be persistent.

## JUDGES 3-4
### Heroes in Crises

Crises and disasters and emergencies often cause ordinary people to rise as heroes. This happened frequently during the times of the judges. It took place with Othniel, Shamgar, Ehud, Deborah, and Barak. God called everyday men and women to arise during dark times and break the yoke of oppression that had their people bound. God still does this today. He knows what's in your heart even better than you do and is able to use you to do astonishing things. Stay close to Him so that you're willing and able to respond when a need arises.

## JUDGES 5; JUDGES 6:1–24
### Where Is God?

---

When the angel of the Lord appeared to Gideon and told him that God was with him, Gideon asked if the Lord was with His people, why had such great disasters happened to them (Judges 6:13). Gideon pointed to the great miracles God had done in the past and asked where He was now. You've probably felt the same way at times. Perhaps problems seem to have a chokehold on your life, and you wonder why God doesn't miraculously liberate you. The problem could be that you don't believe that God is with you.

## Gideon's 300 Men

---

Gideon had an unusual problem: when he went out to war against the invading Midianites, he had *too many* soldiers. God didn't want the Israelites to be able to boast that they'd won the battle in their own might. So He told Gideon to send all but 300 men home. God may strip down your strength and resources at times, leaving you feeling inadequate to face problems or complete a project, but don't despair: with His help you can overcome. He may simply be testing you to see if you fully trust and depend on Him.

## Willing to Help

Gideon and his men routed the Midianites then pursued them. But Gideon's men became faint from hunger, so they stopped at the Israelite town of Sukkoth and asked for food. The people refused to help. They didn't want the Midianites to later retaliate against them. Has something like this ever happened to you? When you're counting on someone to help you in a time of need, it's a body blow if they turn you away instead. But you still need to be able to trust God to help you make it and—unlike Gideon—to forgive those who failed you.

## Mankind's Selfish Wars

---•◦•---

The war between Abimelek and Gaal is a classic example of the confused, proud, and selfish motives driving most of mankind's wars. There are times in today's world when one country is clearly the aggressor and the other is in the right and merely defending itself, but more often than not, both sides are partially right and partially wrong. James 4:1 (KJV) says that fighting and wars come from people's selfish lusts. It's easy to get caught up in emotions when your country is at war, but the Bible says that peacemakers are blessed (Matthew 5:9).

## JUDGES 11–12
### An Anointed Outlaw

———•◦•———

Jephthah was the son of a prostitute, and when his half-brothers kicked him out, he became a raider, and soon he was leading a band of outlaws. He may have seemed like a lowlife, but Jephthah was an anointed orator with powerful leadership skills. This goes to show that you should never judge anyone in haste. The person you're ready to write off may be used mightily of God. This applies to you as well. Don't get discouraged if others look at you with contempt or think of you disparagingly. God is able to use you.

......................................................................

......................................................................

......................................................................

......................................................................

......................................................................

......................................................................

......................................................................

......................................................................

......................................................................

......................................................................

## JUDGES 13–14
### A Strong Man's Weaknesses

———————

Samson is famous for his incredible strength. He's also remembered for his entanglements with the pagan Philistines who were oppressing his people. He reacted in sudden rage, slept with prostitutes, and boasted in pride, yet God still anointed this imperfect hero. You may hope that, like Samson, God will overlook sin in your life and use you anyway. God may continue to bless you while waiting for you to repent, but eventually, you have to turn from your sin and forsake it or, like Samson, suffer the consequences (Proverbs 28:13).

## JUDGES 15–16
### Samson and Delilah

The tragic love affair between Samson and Delilah has become synonymous with men who continue to stay involved in toxic romantic relationships despite the warnings of family and friends—and their own common sense. Some people quip, "The heart wants what the heart wants," but mismatched romances can destroy many other relationships, your reputation, and your finances. Don't get so caught up in feelings of love with your dream person that you refuse to listen to wise counsel and, in the end, learn a bitter lesson at a high price.

## JUDGES 17–18
### Danites on the Move

---

The tribe of Dan, unable to conquer the Canaanites in the fertile valleys, were holed up in the hills. Finally, they decided to migrate far to the north. Much land there had been promised to Israel but was still unclaimed. So they marched north and conquered a city of the Canaanites. Has your current location become too small and cramped for you? Is your present situation just not working out? Has the time come for you to launch forth in some venture? Step out in faith and inherit the promises of God.

## A Horrific Bible Story

Many Christians are stunned when they read the story of the abuse and dismemberment of an Israelite concubine. If you're shocked and disgusted by this story, it shows your heart is in the right place. You *should* be shocked by it. It's reminiscent of the barbaric crimes taking place in the Middle East today. The Bible warns that in the last days evil people will become worse and worse (2 Timothy 3:13), but God never intended such brutal acts to happen. He will see to it that the perpetrators are punished—if not in this life, then in the next.

## Continuing Despite Losses

———•◦•———

God told the Israelite armies to attack the Benjamites, so they did but were badly beaten. Discouraged, they prayed again and were again told to fight. So they did, and a second time the Benjamites crushed them. At this point, most people would have given up, thinking that they hadn't heard from God, but the Israelites trusted the Lord and attacked *again*—and were victorious. It takes great determination and great faith to continue fighting if you've suffered numerous setbacks. But don't give up. Victory often comes only to those who refuse to accept defeat.

# RUTH

Ruth, a Moabite woman, marries into an Israelite family. After all the men of Naomi's family die, Ruth shows loyalty to her aged mother-in-law, Naomi, staying with her and scavenging food in harvest fields to keep them alive. As Ruth gleans barley in a field of wealthy Boaz, Naomi recognizes Boaz as her late husband's relative and encourages Ruth to pursue him as a "kinsman redeemer," one who weds a relative's widow to continue a family line. Sure enough, Boaz marries Ruth, starting a prominent family. One of her descendants is King David, ancestor of Jesus.

## RUTH 1–2
### Uncommon Loyalty

Ruth is an outstanding example of unselfish love, of a person setting aside their rights to personal happiness and fulfilment out of sacrificial love. It would be like you setting aside your rights to life, liberty, and the pursuit of happiness or passing up on an opportunity to enjoy the American dream in order to help another. Perhaps you take on a second job to help your family stay afloat. Perhaps you cancel leisure activities to help care for aged parents. Know that God sees every sacrifice you make, and He will be certain to bless you.

## RUTH 3–4
### Blessed by the Lord

———◦◦———

Before there was any thought of becoming romantically involved, Boaz had blessed Ruth, asking the Lord to repay her work and for a full reward to be given her by the God of Israel, under whose wings she had come for refuge (Ruth 2:12). Not long after, Ruth told Boaz to take her under *his* wing/garment (3:9). You too may pray for God to bless others only to discover that God wants to use *you* to bless them. And don't be surprised if you're blessed in the process. You're blessed when you give (Acts 20:35).

# 1 SAMUEL

Hannah begs God for a son, and after Samuel is born she takes him to the tabernacle to serve God under the aged priest Eli. Samuel later judges Israel, but one day, Israel asks for a king, so God tells Samuel to anoint Saul as king. Saul makes poor choices, so Samuel warns him that he'll be replaced. Saul's successor will be David, who kills a giant named Goliath. The jealous king soon seeks to slay David, who flees for his life. At the end of 1 Samuel, Saul dies battling the Philistines, making way for David to become king.

## 1 SAMUEL 1; 1 SAMUEL 2:1–11
### Dedicating Children

Hannah promised to give her unborn son to God (1 Samuel 1:11), and after he was born, dedicated him to God (vv. 22, 28), becoming a model to millions of Christian parents down through the centuries. Many churches have baby dedication ceremonies where parents devote their young children to God's service. But causing your children to be dedicated to the Lord is more than a one-time ceremony. It involves nearly twenty years of training them in the way that they should go, so that when they are grown, they don't depart from it (Proverbs 22:6).

## Eli's Vile Sons

---

Eli had been a decent high priest, but his sons broke all the rules governing priestly behavior. Eli knew the sins they were involved in but didn't remove them from the priesthood. Like them, he had grown fat eating the choice portions of the sacrifices (1 Samuel 1:29; 4:18). Children can be a tremendous challenge, particularly when they go through a rebellious phase, but it's still your responsibility to train them, applying tough love when needed. There must be consequences for disobedience, especially if their actions hurt others. This won't be enjoyable, but it's necessary.

## Beware the Ark of God

---

The Philistines defeated the Israelites and got their hands on the ark of the covenant. At first, they believed their god was greater than Israel's God, but they changed their mind when Dagon crashed down before the ark and their people began dying of a plague. Never treat the things of God lightly. Avoid speaking disparagingly of Christian leaders. Don't even mock weak Christians, for God's Spirit inhabits them (Romans 14:4, 10). God's Word forbids you to curse others, and doing so may open *your* life to judgment (Matthew 6:15; Romans 12:14).

## Israel Demands a King

Up till this time, the Israelites had been ruled by judges, but they now wanted a king like the nations around them (1 Samuel 8:5). God had anticipated this request (Deuteronomy 17:14–20), but He also knew that the Israelites had lost trust in Him. Likewise, you may want things that are within God's will, but your motives also matter. You may want to marry the first available person, whereas you may be better off to wait. You may want the financial security of a lucrative job, but God may have a more fulfilling career in mind.

## God's Guidance

In 1 Samuel 10:2–6, the prophet Samuel gave Saul an astonishingly detailed idea of the events his day would hold. And it came to pass, just as he predicted. You probably wish that God would give you that kind of foreknowledge of *all* your days. But usually God only gives you just enough lamplight to see the path in front of your feet (Psalm 119:105). And sometimes He's completely silent even though you pray for direction. But you can confidently trust that He's with you just the same. So be patient, and He will guide you.

## Taking Decisive Action

At first, Saul was a decisive, successful king. When the Ammonites threatened to gouge out the eyes of the Israelites of Jabesh-gilead, Saul commanded all Israel to join him—or else! Saul then led them in a predawn attack and utterly defeated the Ammonites. There is much to be said for bold, decisive action. Oftentimes it's the difference between success and failure. Proverbs tells us that the fearful flee from their own shadow while the righteous are bold as a lion (Proverbs 28:1). You may not feel righteous, but if your *cause* is righteous, you'll win.

# 1 SAMUEL 13; 1 SAMUEL 14:1–23
## Jonathan's Bold Attack

Saul's son Jonathan was a mighty warrior with great faith in God. He believed that God could win a battle with many men or with few (1 Samuel 14:6). So just he and his armor-bearer climbed a cliff and attacked a garrison of some twenty Philistines, who were armed to the teeth. You may be outnumbered by your foes, or they may be far more powerful, or you may feel overwhelmed by an enormous task, but don't be afraid. Don't give up in despair. God is with you. And if He's with you, you can overcome.

## 1 SAMUEL 14:24–15:11
### Avoid People-Pleasing

———•———

God had given King Saul very specific instructions regarding the wicked Amalekites and their livestock. But Saul's men wanted to keep the best of the flocks and herds and to spare the Amalekite king. Saul was afraid to contradict them, so he went along with them (1 Samuel 15:24). People-pleasing has been a problem down through the ages (see John 12:42–43). It can hold you back from doing what God wants you to do. Determine in your heart to honor and obey God above all, no matter how unpopular it makes you with people.

## A Heart after God

After Saul disobeyed God one too many times, God told him He'd taken the kingdom from him and given it to someone better (1 Samuel 15:28). But how was David better than Saul? After all, he sinned too. Yes, but David passionately loved God and always repented. He was a man after His own heart (13:14). Do you passionately love God? Do you quickly and wholeheartedly repent when you stumble? Or has your love for God cooled down over the years (Revelation 2:4)? What can you do to restore your first love?

# 1 SAMUEL 17
## Trying Something Crazy

When David realized that, rather than protecting him, King Saul's armor would only slow him down and doom him, he jettisoned it, choosing to face the giant with only a sling and some stones. As he raced toward Goliath, he drove a rock into his forehead. You often can't resolve some problems with conventional wisdom. When you follow God, you might find yourself discarding standard approaches to try something "crazy." But God's kind of crazy works when nothing else will. If you're stuck, pray for a solution. Then do what God shows you.

# 1 SAMUEL 18–19
## A Very Bad Boss

King Saul was a nightmare boss. He often disobeyed God, killed innocent people, and fell into deep, dark depression that only David's music could lift him out of. In addition, he was paranoid, had a quick temper, and tried to kill David on multiple occasions. Be thankful that your boss isn't *that* bad! But he may still be a handful. You may have to pray constantly for the right things to say to soothe his troubled mind. But God can inspire you. The apostle Peter urges believers to obey even cruel masters (1 Peter 2:18).

## 1 SAMUEL 20–21

### Loyal, Supportive Friends

———•◦•———

Jonathan and David had a special bond (1 Samuel 18:1; 2 Samuel 1:26). Jonathan was a loyal friend to David and warned him that his father, Saul, was out to kill him. Jonathan was in line for the throne but gave up his claim when he learned that David was God's choice (1 Samuel 23:16–17). Now, *that's* a true friend! Strive to be that kind of friend to others. Don't just be pals when they're watching your back or helping you fulfill your dreams. Be willing to do the same for them.

# 1 SAMUEL 22–23
## Forgiving and Moving On

The Philistines were attacking the city of Keilah and stealing their grain. God told David and his men to go rescue them, so they did. But when King Saul headed to Keilah, God warned David that Keilah would hand him over to Saul. Thanks, guys! You know how that feels if people have done similar things to you. Despite the good you've done for them, they buckle under pressure to speak against you and even betray you. You need to forgive them and move on. Let God deal with them. You follow Him.

### David Patiently Trusts God

———•◦•———

Two times David had an opportunity to kill Saul to clear the way for himself to become king, and two times David refused to take Saul's life (1 Samuel 24:1–7; 26:5–11). Many men would have done it, but David was trusting the *Lord* to make him king. That took tremendous patience and went against all traditional logic. If you're believing God to do great things in your life, resist the temptation to "help" Him if it means breaking the rules. God has the power to bring about His will. Can you trust Him to act?

........................................................................................

........................................................................................

........................................................................................

........................................................................................

........................................................................................

........................................................................................

........................................................................................

........................................................................................

........................................................................................

........................................................................................

## Abigail's Wisdom

---•◦•---

When a wise, beautiful woman named Abigail learned that her churlish husband had refused to help David and his men, she quickly took several donkeys loaded with food to them. God anointed her, and she spoke prophetically of David becoming king. What do you do if you hear about someone being insulted and slighted? Do you seek to make amends? What if you become aware that someone was underpaid or shortchanged? Do you try to set things right? God rewarded Abigail by making her David's queen. God is able to reward you too.

# 1 SAMUEL 27–28
## Dangerous Spirits

---

In his early days when he was zealous for God, Saul had banned all mediums from Israel (1 Samuel 28:3, 9). Later, he became desperate for spiritual guidance, and since God wasn't speaking to him, he went to a medium at Endor. Sadly, some modern believers and nominal Christians also slip away and seek direction from mediums, psychics, and spiritists. Don't do it. God condemns such occult practices (1 Chronicles 10:13; Isaiah 8:19). If the Lord isn't giving you clear guidance, continue to seek His face until He does.

# 1 SAMUEL 29–31
## In the Pit of Despair

David and his men had left their wives, children, and livestock safely at Ziklag—so they thought—when they went off to war. When they returned, everything was gone, and they wept bitterly. How would you react in such a bleak situation? Would you collapse in defeat, seek someone to blame, or trust God to do the impossible? David turned to God, who told him to pursue the raiders, promising that he'd recover everything. Don't despair. You might not have much hope to go on, but look to God during calamities. He's always there.

# 2 SAMUEL

When King Saul dies, David is crowned king of Judah. After the death of Saul's son, who ruled the northern tribes, David becomes ruler of all Israel. Capturing Jerusalem, David creates a new capital for his unified nation, and God promises David that his throne will be established forever. Military victories make Israel strong, but one spring, David commits adultery with Bathsheba then has her husband murdered. The prophet Nathan confronts David, he repents, and God forgives his sins. Later, however, David's son Absalom conspires to steal the kingdom. When Absalom dies in battle, David reasserts his kingship.

## 2 SAMUEL 1–2
### *Partial Answers to Prayer*

—————•◦•—————

After Saul died in battle against the Philistines, David was crowned king. . .*of Judah* (2 Samuel 2:4). For seven years, David ruled only his own tribe and was engaged in a hard-fought war with Saul's son, Ish-Bosheth, to be king over all Israel (2:10–11). Sometimes God only partially answers your prayers at first—leaving you to fight for the rest of the fulfillment. You wonder why God didn't finish the *entire* job while He was at it. Well, He often does things this way to teach you trust and patience and to toughen you.

## 2 SAMUEL 3–4
### Bitterness and Revenge

Many Israelites died in the civil war, but their families learned to let go and reconcile when the kingdom reunited. But Joab never forgave Abner for killing his brother, Asahel (2 Samuel 2:18–23; 3:30), and he murdered Abner in revenge. War is a cruel thing, and many people have difficulty living at peace with those they once battled. In fact, you may even have difficulty forgiving someone who gossiped about you years ago. But you must let go of any root of bitterness that's troubling you, or it will ruin you (Hebrews 12:15).

## 2 SAMUEL 5–6
### Touching the Ark

———•◦•———

One day, David decided to bring the ark of the covenant to Jerusalem. He didn't know the right way to move it, so he simply had it loaded on an oxcart. A man put out his hand to steady the ark—and was struck dead! (Exodus 25:10–15; 2 Samuel 6:3–7) It's wise to be afraid to "touch the ark." You refrain from meddling in something God is doing because you recognize an anointing on it. Even if it has faults, refrain from trying to "fix" it for fear of hindering God's work. It's good to have such respect.

......................................................................................................

......................................................................................................

......................................................................................................

......................................................................................................

......................................................................................................

......................................................................................................

......................................................................................................

......................................................................................................

......................................................................................................

## 2 SAMUEL 7–8
### God's Covenant with David

One day, a prophet told David that God would give him a lasting dynasty: one of his sons would always sit on the throne of Israel. The last of David's descendants was king in 586 BC, but centuries later, Jesus inherited David's throne. He lives forever, eternally fulfilling this prophecy. Does Jesus rule your heart? You must not only pray for the Spirit of Christ to enter your being and dwell there (Galatians 4:6; Ephesians 3:17), but you must yield to Him daily, be sensitive to Him moment by moment, and obey His commands.

## I've Got Your Back

Once, the Israelites were fighting the Ammonites and Arameans. Joab divided his army and put half under his brother, Abishai. He said if the Ammonites were too strong for Abishai, he'd help him. But if the Arameans were too strong for Joab, Abishai must help him (2 Samuel 10:9–12). Do you have friends you can trust like that? Do they have your back as much as you have theirs? There's tremendous strength in unity (see Ecclesiastes 4:9–10, 12). It's good when fellow believers are able to count on you.

## You Are the Man

---

David committed adultery with Bathsheba then arranged for her husband to be killed. Not long after, the prophet Nathan told David about a rich man who had large flocks but had slain a poor man's only lamb. When David stated that the rich man deserved to die, Nathan informed him that *he* was that man (2 Samuel 12:7). Even today, you may pass judgment on others when you yourself are guilty of similar sins. Jesus commands you not to judge others if you wish to avoid being judged yourself (Matthew 7:1).

## 2 SAMUEL 13; 2 SAMUEL 14:1–11
### Govern Your Desires

David's firstborn son, Amnon, was "in love" with his half sister, Tamar—only it wasn't love. He was merely lusting after her beauty (2 Samuel 13:1, 14–15). Because Amnon failed to rule his passions, he proved himself unfit to rule the kingdom—and died. The patriarch Job had given the safeguard against this 500 years earlier: men are to make a covenant with their eyes to not look lustfully upon women (Job 31:1). Women must also refrain from the wandering eye, looking for illicit relationships (Genesis 39:7–10). Ruling your desires avoids so much trouble.

### Absalom's Conspiracy

---·❖·---

Absalom was very handsome, had five pounds of lovely hair, and was a born orator. For two years, while pretending to be loyal to David, he used flattery to win over the Israelites (2 Samuel 14:25–26; 15:1–5). Finally, he proclaimed himself king. You may know smooth-talkers and deceivers who abuse your trust (Romans 16:18). While you must overcome bitterness toward them, it's wise to learn from the experience and not be taken in again. Don't allow yourself or your loved ones to be deceived by their clever words and persuasive speech.

## Kicked When You're Down

---

Realizing that Absalom's army was marching on Jerusalem, David and his followers evacuated the city, weeping openly (2 Samuel 15:30). A man named Shimei cursed David in this desperate time—yelling at him that he was getting what he deserved (16:5–8). Have you experienced a similar upheaval and rejection—of a lesser magnitude, perhaps? Can you empathize with David's grief and feelings of betrayal? Would you have had the grace and the faith he exhibited in leaving Shimei's bitter tirade in God's hands (vv. 9–13)?

## God Gives Victory

It looked like the end for David, but God was still with him and hadn't abandoned him. Within a matter of days, He had completely ended the threat Absalom had posed. If you've ever confronted desperate situations like this, you'll understand how easy it is to give up in despair. But don't throw in the towel. You may be facing what seems to be overwhelming odds now, but God can turn bleak circumstances around and give you the victory. Lay hold of the promises of God and quote them to yourself when you're tempted to fear.

## An Imperfect Advisor

Joab gave David blunt advice after the battle. Not everything Joab said and did in his life was right, but he sized up *this* situation well (19:1–8). David was making a huge mistake and alienating his followers, but Joab turned the tide. Do you have people whom you trust, who can speak into your life when you're making unwise decisions? You might wish for a counselor with a perfect track record, one who's never made any bonehead mistakes, but chances are you'll get imperfect advisors whom you do well to listen to simply because they're right. . .*this* time.

## Argument at the River

The men of Judah brought David back to his kingdom, and the men of Israel were upset about not being included, so they began arguing. But the men of Judah won the dispute because they argued louder (2 Samuel 19:41–43). But this caused Israel to revolt from David (20:1–2). Have you ever learned this lesson—that sometimes it's not *worth* it to "win" an argument? Even if you feel slighted or your pride is wounded, getting all hot under the collar is not the way to go. Grievous words only stir up anger (Proverbs 15:1).

———•◦•———

Joshua had made a treaty with Amorites called Gibeonites, but Saul broke the treaty and slaughtered them (Joshua 9:15–17; 2 Samuel 21:1–2), so God sent a three-year drought on Israel. Only after making things right with the Gibeonites did Israel enjoy God's blessing again. You may justify treating people unfairly by arguing that they're ungodly, so they don't matter as much as believers. But remember, God loves the godly *and* the ungodly and blesses both with rain and sunshine (Matthew 5:45). If you don't love the ungodly, repent today, and treat them with love.

......................................................................

......................................................................

......................................................................

......................................................................

......................................................................

......................................................................

......................................................................

......................................................................

......................................................................

## 2 SAMUEL 23–24
### The Census and the Plague

You may wonder why God sent a plague on Israel when David conducted a census. Hadn't God ordered Moses to conduct *two* censuses? Yes, He had (Numbers 1:1–2; 26:1–2). But God plainly warned that He'd send a plague if the Israelites didn't do it His way (Exodus 30:12). Today, many Christians think that as long as they're doing good in *most* areas, they can disobey God's other commands—and He will still bless them anyway. He sometimes does wait patiently for a time, but eventually He calls you to repent (Revelation 3:19).

# 1 KINGS

David names Solomon (his son with Bathsheba) his successor, and after David's death, God gives Solomon great wisdom, power, and wealth. He builds God a temple, but in his later years, Solomon's wisdom fails him, for he marries 700 women who turn his heart to idols. When Solomon dies, the ten northern tribes form their own nation under Jeroboam, and the nation of Judah rules in the south. Jeroboam initiates calf worship; many wicked kings follow; and the prophet Elijah confronts Ahab of Israel regarding Baal worship. Judah, meanwhile, has many poor leaders, though some kings follow God.

# 1 KINGS 1
## Stand Up to Pushy People

Adonijah was David's eldest surviving son, so when David was very old, Adonijah decided to declare himself king. David had promised that Bathsheba's young son, Solomon, would be king after him, so Nathan and Bathsheba took quick action to make that happen. It's good to be meek and giving with people, but this doesn't mean allowing them to trample all over you and deny your rights—especially if their actions hinder God's will. Pushy people are always quick to assert their claims, but don't let them bowl you over.

# 1 KINGS 2
## Dispensing Justice, Settling Scores

Not all of David's final instructions to execute or exile people, nor Solomon's subsequent actions, seem gentle and forgiving. But remember that these are frank historical records of biblical kings who were mostly just, frequently merciful, but sometimes personally motivated. Their words and deeds are best understood within the context of their times, an age when kings were the ultimate judges and dispensers of human justice. These accounts aren't intended as guidelines for your interpersonal relationships. For that you have the Sermon on the Mount and Paul's epistles (Matthew 5–7; Romans 12:9–21).

## 1 KINGS 3–4
### What Do You Desire?

What would you ask for if God appeared to you and asked you to name whatever you wanted? Would you ask for wisdom like Solomon or for riches, an attractive mate, or something else? This is the only place in the Bible where God indicated He'd give someone whatever they asked for. Yet many Christians treat God like some genie, thinking that if they simply pronounce their demands and have the faith, He's obligated to give it. But God is sovereign, not your servant, and you're told to pray that *His* will be done on earth (Matthew 6:10).

# 1 KINGS 5–6
## Building the Temple

—◦◦◦—

When King Solomon wanted to build a temple for God, he worked closely with King Hiram of Phoenicia because he needed lumber from his cedar trees. Hiram also sent stonemasons to Israel to cut giant blocks of marble for the temple. Whenever you set out to work on a major project, you do well to seek the advice and expertise of skilled craftsmen—whether they worship God or not. The Phoenicians were Canaanites, but their help was essential in building the temple. You can work with unbelievers without being "unequally yoked" together with them (2 Corinthians 6:14).

# 1 KINGS 7
## King Solomon's Palaces

It took King Solomon seven years to build God's temple; it was 90 feet long, 30 feet wide, and 45 feet high. But it took him thirteen years to build his own palace because it was 150 feet long, 75 feet wide, and 45 feet high (1 Kings 6:2, 38; 7:1–2). He also spent years and much wealth building three more palaces and halls. When you put imagination, passion, and time into God's work, He's usually happy to inspire you in your own dreams and life's work. God desires to bless you abundantly.

## The Ark in the Temple

When the priests brought the ark of the covenant into the newly built temple, the glory of the Lord filled the temple like a thick cloud so that the priests couldn't even stay inside. But glorious as this was, Solomon said that the temple was far too small to contain God (1 Kings 8:10–11, 27). There are holy spots on earth, made holy by the presence of the Spirit, but God is everywhere, so His children can worship Him anywhere on earth (John 4:21–24). What peaceful areas do you often go to and pray?

## Warning on Apostacy

After Solomon prayed and dedicated the temple, God appeared to him a second time. He warned that if His people disobeyed His commands, He'd reject the temple and exile them. Solomon didn't take this to heart, because when he grew old, he turned from God. Watch out that this doesn't happen to you. Are you becoming complacent, losing your love for the Lord, and no longer praying? If you continue on a long, gradual slide away from God, you'll eventually be full of doubts, confused, and lukewarm. Let God renew your heart today.

## 1 KINGS 10; 1 KINGS 11:1–28
### Solomon Backslides

⎯⎯ • ⎯⎯

How could Solomon turn from God—who had appeared to him *twice*? Well, he didn't ever stop believing in God. Rather, his relationship with the Lord was eclipsed by indulging in endless pleasure with pagan wives. Seeking to please them led to compromising his faith. Similar sins still exert their gravitational pull today often beginning with lust. And it's not just the draw of illicit sex. Christians often compromise their faith to avoid being ostracized or persecuted by the world. Any sin—however small in the beginning—has the potential to draw you away from Christ.

## 1 KINGS 11:29-43; 1 KINGS 12
### Idolatry and Revolt

King Solomon led the nation into idolatry, so God caused the northern tribes to revolt against Solomon's son and choose Jeroboam as their king. God promised Jeroboam a lasting dynasty if he would worship Him, but Jeroboam also sinned grievously by setting up golden calves. You may say, "I'd never do that," but you also need to guard against setting up idols in your heart. This can be a constant challenge, because Paul states that greed (covetousness, excessive love for things) is idolatry also (Colossians 3:5). Stay close to God.

....................................................................................

....................................................................................

....................................................................................

....................................................................................

....................................................................................

....................................................................................

....................................................................................

....................................................................................

....................................................................................

....................................................................................

## 1 KINGS 13; 1 KINGS 14:1–18
### A Prophet Warns Jeroboam

God loved His people greatly, so He began sending prophets to warn Judah and Israel to return to Him. An unnamed prophet did miracles before Jeroboam, but though this temporarily got his attention, Jeroboam was soon back to worshipping idols. It's easy to slip into getting your security from money or material things, so dedicate your life afresh to God every morning. Ask Him to tear down any idols that spring up in your heart. It's not a sin to have nice things, but it *is* a sin to put those things before God.

## Pharaoh's Invasion

---

Solomon had covered the temple and his palace with gold and filled them with treasures, including 500 gold shields (1 Kings 10:16–17). Now, with the Israelites divided and fallen into idolatry, Shishak marched north and took all this gold. As long as Christians are united in love and forgive one another, they're protected by prayer, and their spiritual enemy can't get a toehold to enter and rob them. But when God's people allow divisions, refuse to forgive, and become materialistic, their spiritual defenses become weaker, and this allows the enemy to make inroads (John 10:10).

# 1 KINGS 16–17
## Bad Kings, Good Prophet

The northern kingdom, Israel, was ruled by a series of bad kings, culminating in the worst king yet—Ahab. But God loved His people and raised up a prophet named Elijah to boldly speak the truth in this dark hour. You might be tempted to despair at the present state of your nation, but consider the great men and women of God whose voices are raised in these days. God is also calling you to let your light shine so that people can see an example of a life changed by God (Matthew 5:16; Philippians 2:15).

# 1 KINGS 18
## Challenge on Mount Carmel

In the Canaanite pantheon, both El (the true, High God) and Baal (his supposed, chief son) were considered deities. So the Israelites also tried to get away with worshipping both. But Elijah insisted that they choose which one was the true God and love *only* Him (1 Kings 18:21). Your choice today is likely not between God and Baal. You may believe that there's only one God, and Jesus is His Son, but your challenge today is, Do you love Him more than anyone else (Matthew 10:37–39)? Whose opinions do you value more (John 12:42–43)?

## God Meets Elijah

---

After soundly defeating the priests of Baal, Elijah likely expected a revival to sweep the nation. When this didn't happen and instead Jezebel threatened to kill him, the people didn't stand with him, and Elijah became depressed and wanted to die. But God greatly encouraged him. You too may have experienced despair. Perhaps your dreams and high hopes have been dashed, or perhaps you did a great service for others but were attacked or accused instead of being rewarded. But it's not over! God isn't defeated and He isn't done yet. Give Him time and room to act.

## Avoid the Wicked

One day the Arameans attacked Israel and were defeated in battle. But instead of killing their king and ending the threat, Ahab made a trade treaty with him (1 Kings 20:34, 41–42). A prophet told Ahab that in entering into this agreement, he had forfeited his life. A modern proverb warns, "If you run with wolves, you'll learn to howl." The New Testament tells Christians not to join in the world's evil ways (2 Corinthians 6:17; 1 Peter 4:3–4). You may have to do business with them, but don't form close partnerships with them.

# 1 KINGS 22
## Disaster Seeks Evil People

———•◦•———

God promises that if His people love and obey Him, blessings will pursue and overtake their lives (Deuteronomy 28:2). But disaster will just as surely pursue and overtake the disobedient. God used one "random, stray" arrow to end Ahab's life (1 Kings 22:34). What were the odds of *that*? The Bible warns you that your sin will certainly find you out (Numbers 32:23). So be quick to repent and obtain forgiveness. The Lord is always ready to forgive. Why trust a lucky rabbit's foot to ward off evil? Call out to the Lord to protect you.

# 2 KINGS

The story of 2 Kings continues with more bad rulers, a few good ones, and the ultimate loss of the two nations. Elijah's successor, Elisha, performs many miracles in northern Israel. Its rulers are wicked, and Israel's last king, Hoshea, is carried away into Assyria (2 Kings 17:6) in 722 BC. Judah, with occasional good kings, lasts longer, but in 586 BC its capital of Jerusalem falls to the Babylonians (25:3–4, 8–10). Besides taking everything valuable, the Babylonians deport thousands of captives (24:11). A new Babylonian king promotes Jehoiachin, the last real king of Judah, to a place of honor in his court (24:27–30).

### Learning from Elijah

---

Elisha knew that God was about to carry Elijah up to heaven, and so Elisha refused to leave his side. Elisha then asked for a double anointing of Elijah's power after he was gone, and he received exactly that. The Lord will often have you spend years learning from older men or women of God, and the purpose of that is to strengthen you and cause you to mature and become wiser so that one day you'll be able to take responsibility and teach others in turn. Take advantage of every opportunity now to learn.

## 2 KINGS 3; 2 KINGS 4:1–17
### The Widow's Oil

———•◦•———

One day a young prophet died, leaving behind a wife and two young sons. They had no food or money—only a little olive oil. So Elisha told the widow to gather many jars and pour the oil into them. Miraculously, the oil kept flowing until she ran out of jars (2 Kings 4:1–7). God still does miracles today, and He still rewards you in proportion to your faith. When He tells you to gather many jars in anticipation of the increase He's about to send, gather *many*. When He tells you to launch out in faith, take large steps.

Naaman had come to Elisha to be healed, and he expected a dramatic ceremony, but Elisha didn't even come outside to see him. He simply sent out a messenger telling him to bathe in the Jordan. Proud Naaman was indignant. However, his servants finally persuaded him to do it. You too may have a need—*and* a preconceived idea of how God ought to meet that need. It will probably be a way that shows you great favor and respect. But God also knows that you may need humility as much as you need healing.

## 2 KINGS 6; 2 KINGS 7:1–11
### Miracle for the Desperate

The Aramean army was besieging Samaria, and people were starving. But Elisha informed them that the following morning they would have an abundance of food to eat. Some people doubted this could happen—but it did! After you've been stuck in a bleak situation for months, it can be hard to believe that God even *wants* to do a miracle—let alone can. But God looks on humble hearts full of faith and answers accordingly. He's still loving and caring, and He's still all-powerful. What miracle do you need? Can you trust God for it?

## Finishing a To-Do List

The Lord had told Elijah to anoint Hazael as king of Aram, Jehu as king of Israel, and Elisha as a prophet in his place (1 Kings 19:15–16). Elijah only did the *third* thing. It was left to Elisha to carry out the first and second instructions (2 Kings 8:7–15; 9:1–3). Sometimes, you're not able to finish all your goals before you die, and others have to carry on what you started. Are you leaving things in good order so they can pick up where you left off? Have you shared your vision with the next generation?

## The Dog of War

Jehu was a ruthless killer who conducted bloody campaigns to wipe out his enemies. He slew two kings, one queen, seventy princes, forty-two royals, and scores of pagan priests. He was doing what God told him to do, but his descendants slaughtered people without such instructions (Hosea 1:4). This goes to show that just because someone is allowed to do something, doesn't mean you have permission to follow in their footsteps. Be very certain that any unusual actions you engage in are authorized and sanctioned.

## Overthrowing the Wicked

Athaliah was the mother of Azariah, king of Judah. After Azariah died, she murdered all her royal grandchildren then became queen. But seven years later, the high priest pulled his own coup, had that wicked witch killed, and declared Prince Joash king. Sometimes evil seems to be triumphant, good people are oppressed, and the truth is suppressed. But never lose hope in the power of good to overcome in the end. If God is with you, who can be against you? Nevertheless, it may take wisdom, courage, and much prayer to prevail.

## 2 KINGS 12–13
### Elisha's Quiet Years

———•◦•———

Elisha was last seen in action in Damascus about 843 BC (2 Kings 8:7). Then he disappeared for some forty-five years, only to reappear a final time during the reign of King Jehoash (2 Kings 13:14–20), when he was on his deathbed. And he was still prophesying! You too may have "quiet years" when, judging by outward results at least, you feel you aren't doing or accomplishing much. But let God be the judge of that. Faithful, quiet service is of great value in His eyes (1 Thessalonians 4:11; 1 Timothy 2:2).

## 2 KINGS 14; 2 KINGS 15:1–22
### God Pities the Disobedient

---

Jeroboam II became king of Israel (the northern kingdom) at a time when it was being overrun by the Arameans, and the Israelites were suffering bitterly. God pitied them and helped Jeroboam II drive out the enemy, even though he was an idol worshipper (2 Kings 14:23–27). You may have the idea that God has absolutely no compassion for the suffering of those who don't walk in the light, close to Him, in total obedience. But Jesus tells us that God cares even for evil and utterly thankless people (Matthew 5:44–45). So you should care for them too.

## Trusting the Assyrians

When Israel and Aram prepared to attack Judah, instead of asking God for help, King Ahaz stripped all the silver and gold from God's temple, sent it to the king of Assyria, and told him, "I'm your slave! Save me!" (2 Kings 16:5–9) You can be thankful when *God* gives you loyal friends and allies who stand up for you, but if you ignore Him and only depend on powerful people to save you, it can actually make the situation worse. Ahaz's son, Hezekiah, would have nothing but trouble from the Assyrians (see Psalm 146:3).

## Israel Cast Out

The northern kingdom soon became a vassal of the Assyrian empire, and when they tried to rebel, the Assyrians deported them. God allowed it. Why? Because the Israelites had worshipped worthless idols until they themselves had become worthless (2 Kings 17:15). You become *like* the object of your worship. This can also be a positive thing. Second Corinthians 3:18 says that as you faithfully contemplate the Lord's glory, you yourself will be transformed into His image with ever-increasing glory. And 1 John 3:2 states that when Christ returns, those who love Him shall be like Him.

## 2 KINGS 18:17–19:19
### Looking to God

King Hezekiah had the right reaction when the Assyrians threatened Judah and mocked God (2 Kings 19:1, 14). He went straight to the temple, poured out his heart to God, and looked to Him for deliverance. When trouble comes, many people, rather than standing their ground, give in to the "flight" side of the "fight or flight" instinct, and flee as a bird to a distant mountain. But as David asked, how could he follow the advice of those who told him to flee? After all, he had put his trust in the Lord (Psalm 11:1).

## Hezekiah's Life Extended

---

When King Hezekiah became very sick, God candidly told him that he was going to die (2 Kings 20:1). That didn't seem to leave Hezekiah any wiggle room, but when he cried out with tears, God relented and told him he'd live another fifteen years. God often relents if people pray wholeheartedly. He states that just as the clay is in the hands of a potter, so people are in His hands (v. 6), but He *also* says that if people repent and change their ways, He revises His plans for their lives accordingly (see Jeremiah 18:6–11).

## 2 KINGS 21–22
### The Tenderhearted King

The Law of Moses had just been found after having gone missing for fifty years, and an official read it to King Josiah. He was tenderhearted and was alarmed when he heard how God would judge His people if they worshipped idols, because that's what Judah had done. How do *you* react when you read a blunt truth in the Bible for the first time? Do you slowly shut your ears until you can no longer hear the conviction of God's Spirit? Or do you take it to heart and repent? Do you change your ways?

# 2 KINGS 23
## Major Housecleaning

There were many idols and pagan altars in the temple, and Josiah removed them like the garbage they were. He destroyed all the idols in Jerusalem and got rid of mediums and pagan priests. He did a major housecleaning throughout the land. Do you need to clean house? Are there any videos or magazines in your home that dishonor the Lord? Do you watch any TV shows that promote ungodly values? You'll have to use great wisdom and not just storm into your teenagers' bedrooms and begin stuffing their belongings into trash bags. Pray for conviction *and* wisdom.

## The Fall of Judah

———•◦•———

Because Josiah repented, God kept judgment from falling in his day. But most of the later kings were idolaters, so the guilty verdict couldn't be delayed forever. The threatened judgments of Deuteronomy 28:15–68 finally came due. Actions always have consequences, and though God's train may seem to be running late—and you're tempted to think it will never arrive—the day will come when it finally pulls into the station. And nobody should be surprised. God still judges both individuals and nations. However, He often delays His punishment if the righteous cry out to Him.

# 1 CHRONICLES

Chronicles are largely a repeat of Kings but with an emphasis almost entirely on the southern kingdom of Judah. Almost all mentions of the northern kingdom are dropped, while the history of Judah is explored in greater detail. In the eleventh chapter, 1 Chronicles turns to the story of David, with special emphasis on his leadership in worshipping God. This book emphasizes the temple in Jerusalem and describes the preparations David made for building God's house. Another important focus is on God's promise that David would have an eternal line through his descendants; this is fulfilled in Jesus Christ.

# 1 CHRONICLES 1–2
## Endless Genealogies

Here come the lengthy genealogical lists you've been dreading. But within these lists of names are some sparkling gems. For example, 1 Chronicles 2:34 tells us that an Israelite named Sheshan had no sons, only daughters. But he had an Egyptian servant named Jarha to whom he gave a daughter in marriage. Proverbs 29:21 states that he who favors a servant shall, in the end, have him for a son. Sheshan certainly found this to be true. In a similar way, even though you were once far from God's kingdom, the Lord has now adopted you.

# 1 CHRONICLES 3-4
## Better Late Than Never

---

Most of the twelve tribes had conquered the Canaanites and settled down in their place in Joshua's day, centuries earlier. But several Simeonite clans only took their land during King Hezekiah's reign, 750 years later (1 Chronicles 4:34–43). You may be a late bloomer as well and feel far behind others of your generation who are already married and settled into a career. But don't despair. God can still do great things in your life. With His help, many who are first shall be last, and others who are last shall be first (Matthew 20:16).

# 1 CHRONICLES 5; 1 CHRONICLES 6:1–49
## More Genealogy Gems

The tribe of Reuben, of Gad, and the half-tribe of Manasseh waged war against the Hagrites. God delivered the Hagrites and all their vast flocks and herds into their hands because they prayed to God during the battle (1 Chronicles 5:18–22). Have you looked into your family's genealogical records and learned anything amazing? Have you heard stories of ancestors who did unusual things? It should come as no surprise. God has enabled otherwise ordinary people to do exploits down through history because they prayed.

## Misfortune in the Family

---•◦•---

After the Israelites moved to Egypt, Ephraim's two sons went up to Gath to steal cattle and were killed. Though it was their own fault, Ephraim mourned for them many days. He named his next son Beriah, meaning "misfortune," because there had been misfortune in his family. It seems that almost every family has a sad tale to tell— either of an accident, an illness, or a death. Sometimes it's clear where the fault lies, but other times it can be difficult to understand why God allows such troubles. But when you cross over that final Jordan, you'll understand.

## Phinehas the Gatekeeper

Levites called gatekeepers guarded the entrance to the Tabernacle. The most famous gatekeeper was Phinehas, and 1 Chronicles 9:19–20 says that the Lord was with him. Phinehas once impaled a wicked couple with a spear (Numbers 25:6–10) and stopped a plague from spreading. Some people take their jobs for God very seriously, and as a result, God blesses them mightily. These days, Christians generally don't fight with physical weapons but battle the forces of evil with spiritual arms (2 Corinthians 10:3–5). How zealous are *you* for God?

# 1 CHRONICLES 10–11
## David's Mighty Men

———— ·•·‣ ————

David had an elite group of super warriors, crack troops who did great exploits. They took on lions, monster-men, and entire armies, and it seemed that nothing could stop them. Small wonder David put one of them in charge of his personal bodyguard (see 1 Chronicles 11:10–25). There are mighty men and women of God today as well, who through prayer and bold, sacrificial action, carve out whole regions for the kingdom of God. Many spiritual mighty men are listed in Hebrews 11. Are you willing for God to make *you* mighty in spirit?

## Can I Trust You?

---

When Saul and his army were hunting David to kill him, some Benjamites—Saul's own relatives—defected to David. When they first showed up, David wasn't sure he could trust them, but Amasai gave such a rousing pledge of loyalty that it convinced David (1 Chronicles 12:1–2, 16–18). If you, like David, stand up as a bold, honest witness for Christ, God will touch people's hearts—people whom you might least expect to be moved. Goodhearted people who are tired of selfishness, hypocrisy, and cruelty will come to faith in Christ.

## Mulberry Trees Moving

One time the Philistines invaded Israel, and God instructed David to circle behind them then wait till he heard the wind rustling in the tops of the mulberry trees. That was the sign that God had gone out ahead of David's army (1 Chronicles 14:13–16). Sometimes when you pray, the Lord will impress a thought or a specific Bible passage on your mind, and you may not be sure if it's God leading you or simply your imagination. It pays to be cautious until you're certain. Then, once you're sure you've received God's directions, advance fearlessly.

## Put Up with It for Now

David brought the ark to Jerusalem. Meanwhile, the Tabernacle and God's altar were in Gibeon. David wanted to build a temple to unite worship in Jerusalem. Besides, the ark was in a mere tent. But God put building a temple on hold for the next *thirty-some years*. You too may desire to implement an immediate solution when situations are less than ideal, yet God often isn't in a hurry—even when the project would glorify Him. And make sure that He wants *you* to do a project before you start. He might want someone else to handle it.

# 1 CHRONICLES 18-20
## Tribute from Enemy Kingdoms

Israel had often been oppressed by many of the surrounding kingdoms, so God helped David subjugate all these enemies. Finally, Israel dwelt in peace. A bonus was that David captured much war booty—silver, gold, and bronze—in the process. Proverbs 16:7 says that when a person's ways please the Lord, He makes even their enemies to be at peace with them, so it's in your own self-interest to be sure that you do things that please the Lord. This frequently means obeying God even when you don't feel like it.

---•◦•---

David had been told that he wouldn't be the one to build God's temple, but David still did what he could: he had large stones cut in preparation and set aside much gold, iron, and bronze (1 Chronicles 22:2–5). David even drew up the building plans (28:11–19). If you're not part of God's A-team, that doesn't mean you have *no* part to play. You might not be in the spotlight, making headlines or carrying the ball across the goal line, but you can be an invaluable team member by providing backup and support.

......................................................................................................

......................................................................................................

......................................................................................................

......................................................................................................

......................................................................................................

......................................................................................................

......................................................................................................

......................................................................................................

......................................................................................................

......................................................................................................

# 1 CHRONICLES 23–24
## New Jobs for the Levites

During their desert wanderings, the Levites had been responsible for dismantling the Tabernacle, moving it, then setting it up again (Numbers 4:5–20). Most of the Levites were therefore out of a job after the Tabernacle became stationary in Canaan, so David assigned them new duties (1 Chronicles 23:1–5, 25–32). Circumstances change, and you're wise to change with them if you wish to remain useful and relevant. This is also true when your employment dries up; you need to be able to retool and reinvent yourself in order to continue earning a living.

### Organizing the Levites

David chose some Levites to play musical instruments and sing before the Lord (1 Chronicles 6:31–32; 2 Chronicles 29:25); he organized others as gatekeepers to take turns guarding the Tabernacle (1 Chronicles 9:22; 26:12); he selected others as treasurers, etc. If you wish to get the most out of the team you work with, you need to be organized, follow schedules, and practice good time management principles. Things get done in an efficient manner when everyone knows their duties, does their fair share, and starts and ends their shift on time.

# 1 CHRONICLES 27; 1 CHRONICLES 28:1-9
## Final Advice to Solomon

---•◦•---

After choosing Solomon to be king after him, the aged David admonished him to serve God with wholehearted devotion. He assured Solomon that if he sought God, he would be sure to find Him; but if he forsook God, the Lord would not be there to help him (1 Chronicles 28:9). This verse boils the plan for a successful life down to its simplest essence, and millions of Christians can testify how true this is. Seek God before you begin your day, during the day's peace or problems, and in the evening.

## Inspiring Others to Give

As soon as he received great riches, David dedicated much of it to the Lord (1 Chronicles 29:1–2). Then, years later, he again gave generously to the cost of building God's temple. This put him in a position to challenge others to give also (vv. 3–9). You may think that you can't give generously because you don't have great riches, but Jesus proved that wrong when He praised a poor widow for giving just two small coins (Mark 12:41–44). Give what you can to worthy causes that your church is involved in.

# 2 CHRONICLES

Second Chronicles continues the emphasis that 1
Chronicles has on Judah. David's son Solomon is made
king, builds the temple, and becomes one of the most
prominent rulers ever. But when he dies, the nation
divides. Then the various kings of the southern kingdom of Judah are profiled down to the destruction of
Jerusalem by the Babylonians. Extra information—such
as the repentance of evil King Manasseh—that isn't in
2 Kings, appears, filling in many gaps in our knowledge. This book ends with the Persian king Cyrus
allowing the Jews to rebuild their devastated temple.

## 2 CHRONICLES 1–3
### God Doesn't Dwell in Temples

———•❖•———

Solomon prepared to build a temple but admitted that no one could build a temple big enough to contain God (2 Chronicles 2:6; 6:18). Nevertheless, God put His Name there, looked down from heaven, and heard His people's prayers (6:20–21). Sometimes He appeared as a glory cloud filling the temple. Today God longs to dwell in your heart, not in buildings of dead stone and stained-glass windows (Acts 7:48). If you already have the Spirit in your heart, make room for even *more* of God's power and glory.

# 2 CHRONICLES 4–5; 2 CHRONICLES 6:1–11
## Bronze Bulls, Big Basin

---

In front of God's temple was an enormous bronze basin, thirty feet in circumference, resting on the backs of twelve huge bronze bulls—symbols of the twelve tribes. God's instructions to Moses for building the Tabernacle had made no mention of these, so David must have been directly inspired by God when writing instructions for the craftsmen. God still uses creative people's knowledge and imaginations to bring glory to Him—everything from creating songs, books, and plays, to paintings, sculptures, and movies. How do you use *your* imagination to make the Gospel appealing and to glorify God?

## 2 CHRONICLES 6:12–7:16
### *Prayer of Dedication*

Solomon knelt before the temple and publicly prayed to God, asking Him to hear whenever His people prayed to Him, whether to ask for deliverance from a drought, a famine, an epidemic, or a grasshopper plague; for help fighting enemies, or for forgiveness of sins. These days, you don't need to go to a temple to pray, nor do you have to even kneel facing in the *direction* of a temple (John 4:20–24). If you have the Spirit living in your heart, you can cry out to God wherever you are, and He will hear you.

## The Queen of Sheba

One day a queen came to Jerusalem from the distant land of Sheba (modern Yemen); she had heard of Solomon's great wisdom and wealth and came to ask him many questions. She very likely also came to establish a lucrative trade treaty. These days, many people come to America from distant nations to find a better life. While your natural tendency might be to shy away from strangers, this gives you terrific opportunities to share the Gospel with different people groups. Jesus said that He was greater than Solomon (Luke 11:31), so tell others about Him.

## 2 CHRONICLES 10–12
### A Foolish Answer

———•◦•———

Have you ever been asked a question, and though you didn't really know what to respond, felt compelled by pride to give an authoritative answer? Rehoboam did. When the northern tribes asked him to lighten the financial burden his father, Solomon, had imposed, Rehoboam boasted that he'd make their lives even *more* miserable. You may think that others have no choice but to do what you say, but beware: they could rebel, and you could lose it all. So pray before you answer, get wise counsel, pray again, and have humility when you speak.

................................................................................

................................................................................

................................................................................

................................................................................

................................................................................

................................................................................

................................................................................

................................................................................

................................................................................

................................................................................

## 2 CHRONICLES 13–15
### God Is on Your Side

———

One day there was war between Israel and Judah. King Abijah of Judah warned Israel not to fight them, that God was with them because Judah was true to God. Sure enough, the armies fought, and Israel suffered a massive defeat. This principle still holds true today. If you love God and are obeying His commands, He has promised to be with you to fight for you and defend you. Your enemies may have all the advantages, and you may feel you're just a weakling, but trust that you have a powerful God on your side.

## 2 CHRONICLES 16–17;
## 2 CHRONICLES 18:1–17
### Learning God's Law

———

Jehoshaphat was true to the Lord, so God mightily blessed him and strengthened him (2 Chronicles 17:3–6). Jehoshaphat very wisely sent Levites with the Book of the Law to all the towns of Judah to teach the people about God (vv. 8–9). This turned many back to Him (19:4). Christians must also realize the importance of people reading and understanding God's Word. Do you read the Bible to your children and make sure they have age-appropriate translations? Do you support your church and its Sunday school programs? If not, start today.

## 2 CHRONICLES 18:18–20:26
### The Battle Is God's

————— ·•·• —————

When an alliance of three enemy nations invaded Judah, a Levite named Jahaziel told King Jehoshaphat not to be afraid because of this vast army. For the battle was not his, but God would fight for him (2 Chronicles 20:15). And God *did* do a great miracle! It can be difficult to trust that the Lord is going to come through for you when the outlook is bleak and it appears that the end has come. But don't give up hope. God hasn't rejected you or abandoned you, and He's still capable of doing miracles.

## 2 CHRONICLES 20:27–37;
## 2 CHRONICLES 21–22
### Areas of Compromise

---

Jehoshaphat was a godly king. However, the Lord was angry that Jehoshaphat had made military and trade alliances with Ahab of Israel (2 Chronicles 19:1–3; 20:35–37). He'd even arranged for his son Jehoram to marry the idolatrous Athaliah, daughter of Ahab and Jezebel (21:1, 6). Many people today, although they're personally godly, have entered into alliances with wicked people. This is to their own detriment, because while God is able to bless *most* areas of their lives, He withholds His blessing from areas of compromise. Hand every part of your life over to God.

## A Skillfully Executed Coup

When it came time to depose evil Queen Athaliah, the high priest showed the rightful ruler, Prince Joash, to the nobles of Judah and had them swear loyalty. Then, during the changing of the temple guard, when troop strength was at its highest, he staged a daring coup. You need to be more than righteous to succeed in life; you also need to be wise. This is true in most ventures: if you insist on chopping wood with a dull ax, you have to work a lot harder. Use a little wisdom: sharpen your ax first (Ecclesiastes 10:10).

## 2 CHRONICLES 25–26
### Slipping into Darkness

With God's help, King Amaziah conquered Edom. But then he brought the idols of their gods back to Jerusalem and worshipped them. A prophet asked Amaziah why he worshipped gods who couldn't even save the Edomites from *him*. Christians today sometimes do something similar. They originally became weary of astrology and fortune-tellers because they provided no real answers or peace. Yet after they have come to Christ, they turn back and dabble in their old superstitions to get guidance (Isaiah 8:19; Galatians 4:8–11). Don't slip back into pagan superstition and darkness.

## The Good Samaritans

———•———

The Israelite army invaded Judah and took 200,000 captives and much booty to Samaria. But a prophet named Oded warned them that if they did this, God's fierce anger would burn against them. So the Samaritans returned all the captives to Judah, giving them food, water, clothes, medicine, and donkeys. Many times, even worldly, unsaved people have a conscience and do what's honest and right. How much more should Christians do the right thing and not be negligent in showing compassion? Is there a wrong you need to make right? Do you need to apologize to someone?

...................................................................................................................

...................................................................................................................

...................................................................................................................

...................................................................................................................

...................................................................................................................

...................................................................................................................

...................................................................................................................

...................................................................................................................

## 2 CHRONICLES 29:12–30:12
### New Instructions

In Hezekiah's day, while the priests sacrificed bulls, rams, goats, and lambs in obedience to the Law of Moses, the Levites did something totally new. They played instruments and sang David's psalms—as specified by David and the prophets (2 Chronicles 29:20–30). Many people today are so set in following old ways of doing things and aren't open to new, improved methods and joyful traditions. But you can miss out on some very beautiful and enriching things that way. Why not try something new? Bring some joy into your worship!

## 2 CHRONICLES 30:13–27; 2 CHRONICLES 31
### Unlawful but Joyful Celebrations

---

God allowed the Israelites to celebrate the Passover even though most hadn't purified themselves (2 Chronicles 30:18–20). Plus, they celebrated Passover for an extra week even though that simply wasn't the way things were done (v. 23). God wanted people to obey the Law, but He wasn't a legalist. Jesus taught that God desired mercy and love even if that meant doing without sacrificial offerings (Matthew 12:7). God allowed the Law to be broken in emergencies (Luke 6:3–4). He is and always has been more interested in sincere worship than outward rituals.

The besieging Assyrians mocked God and told the Jews not to trust Him. But when Hezekiah and Isaiah prayed, God sent an angel into the enemy camp, who killed 185,000 men. The Assyrians abruptly broke off their siege (2 Kings 18:33–35; 19:35; 2 Chronicles 32:13–21). Many people doubt that an angel could kill 185,000 men in one night—until you remind them that the angel probably spread a deadly plague. It was still a miracle, however, even if God used a natural phenomenon. The plague wouldn't have happened if Hezekiah and Isaiah hadn't prayed.

## 2 CHRONICLES 33:20–25; 2 CHRONICLES 34
### Making Life Changes

———•◦•———

King Josiah began seeking the Lord when he was sixteen; when he was twenty, he began demolishing pagan idols and altars throughout Israel; and when he was twenty-six, he started repairing God's temple (2 Chronicles 34:1–8). If you've drifted away from God, the first thing you must do is discover Him anew. Once you know Him, He convicts you to get rid of things in your life that displease Him (see Jeremiah 1:10). But you must also then fill those spaces with the things of God and spend time with other believers, rebuilding your faith.

...............................................................................................

...............................................................................................

...............................................................................................

...............................................................................................

...............................................................................................

...............................................................................................

...............................................................................................

...............................................................................................

...............................................................................................

...............................................................................................

## 2 CHRONICLES 35–36
### Avoid Meddling

King Josiah was leading all Judah and even long-backslidden Israel back to God. But when Pharaoh's armies marched up the coast to fight the Babylonians, Josiah decided to go out and stop them. Pharaoh told Josiah to mind his own business, but Josiah refused to. . .and was killed needlessly. There's a shortage of men and women serving God, so it's a tragedy when you love God passionately but get sidetracked in matters that you shouldn't. It can derail your usefulness and service for God. So stay focused on Him.

# EZRA

About a half century after the Babylonians sacked
Jerusalem and carried the Jews into captivity, the
Babylonian Empire has collapsed, and Persia is the
new world power. King Cyrus allows a group of
Jewish exiles to return to their homeland, Judah, to
rebuild their temple. Some 42,000 people return
and resettle the land. About seventy years later, Ezra
is part of a smaller group that returns. Ezra teaches
God's law to the people, who have fallen away from
God to the point that they're intermarrying with
pagans, something that was strictly forbidden by
Moses (Deuteronomy 7:1–3).

## EZRA 1–2
### Choosing to Return

———◆———

King Cyrus of Persia allowed all Jews to return to Judah to restore their nation and rebuild God's temple, but only 42,360 chose to go (Ezra 2:1–2, 64). Most Jews were now comfortable in foreign lands; had careers, property, and businesses, and didn't want to uproot and go. This same tendency of inertia keeps many Christians from boldly stepping out and following the Lord today. That's why Jesus sweetened the offer and promised that whoever forsook loved ones, houses, or lands would receive a hundredfold more in return—*and* enjoy glorious eternal life (Matthew 19:29).

## EZRA 3–4
### Refusing Bad Fellowship

———◆———

When the Samaritans heard that the Jews were rebuilding God's temple, they offered to help, claiming that they revered God too. They wanted access to the temple once it was rebuilt. But the Jews refused because the Samaritans worshipped other gods also (Ezra 4:1–3; 2 Kings 17:23–41). The New Testament says that if someone doesn't follow the true teachings of Christ, they don't know God, and believers shouldn't fellowship with them (2 John 1:9–10). Don't be judgmental about it, but refuse to become entangled with those who don't honor Christ.

## EZRA 5–6
### Insist on Your Rights

When asked by what authority they were building God's temple, the Jews informed King Darius that they had received permission from a former Persian ruler. Darius made a search and found that original letter of authorization, so he supported the Jews' endeavor. The apostle Paul also insisted on his rights as a Roman citizen (Acts 16:37–39; 22:25–29). Today, it's important that you know that freedom of religion and freedom of speech are enshrined in the laws of this land, so insist on these rights and freedoms, and don't allow anyone to rob you of them.

## EZRA 7–8
## The Hand of the Lord

———— ·•· ————

Ezra twice mentioned the hand of the Lord being upon him (Ezra 7:28; 8:22). By this he meant that God's favor and blessing and protection were on his life. The Bible says the hand of the Lord upholds those who fall (Psalm 37:24; 63:8) and strengthens believers (Isaiah 41:10). God's Word says that He opens His hand to supply your needs (Psalm 145:14–16). Is the hand of God upon your life? Yes, even when you go through hard times, or you're impatiently waiting for answers to prayer. God will do good to you eventually.

# EZRA 9–10
## Rules Regarding Marriage

God had warned the Israelites not to intermarry with the Canaanites because those idolaters would lead His people away from Him. In Ezra's day, Jewish men were marrying idol-worshipping women, so Ezra had them divorce those wives. Likewise, in New Testament times, Christians are admonished to marry only fellow believers. If unmarried, you shouldn't marry an unbeliever (1 Corinthians 7:39; 2 Corinthians 6:14–15). However, if you're already married to a non-Christian, you shouldn't seek a divorce. After all, you might eventually win them to Christ (1 Corinthians 7:12–16).

# NEHEMIAH

Nehemiah serves as the king's cupbearer (Nehemiah 1:11), a trusted servant who tastes the king's wine to ensure that it isn't poisoned. Nehemiah lives in Susa, the capital of the Persian empire. He's disturbed to learn that the exiles in Judah haven't yet rebuilt Jerusalem's walls, knocked down by the Babylonians. Nehemiah receives the king's permission to return there, where he leads a team of builders—against much pagan opposition—in reconstructing the walls in only fifty-two days. The quick work on the project shocks the Jews' enemies, who perceive that God has empowered His people (6:16).

# NEHEMIAH 1–2
## When God Favors You

Nehemiah needed an extended leave from the palace, but getting away for any length of time seemed out of the question. So Nehemiah prayed for God to give him favor with the king—and God did precisely that (Nehemiah 2:6–8). Do you have an urgent need? Are you involved in a project that requires the approval of your boss or government officials? Are you being hindered by red tape and bureaucracy? Read verses such as Philippians 4:19, which state that God shall supply your needs, then believe that He will act on your behalf.

## NEHEMIAH 3–4
### Building Despite Opposition

———•◦•———

Nehemiah led the project to rebuild Jerusalem's walls, and many Jews dropped what they were doing and helped. Even the daughters of a ruler named Shallum, together with their father, did their share. But certain nobles refused to put their shoulders to the work (Nehemiah 3:5, 12). When your church is engaged in a united project, the work will get done quicker if everyone helps—in whatever way they can. Even if your schedule or health won't permit you to get directly involved, you can give financially or pray for the project's success.

....................................................................................

....................................................................................

....................................................................................

....................................................................................

....................................................................................

....................................................................................

....................................................................................

....................................................................................

....................................................................................

....................................................................................

## NEHEMIAH 5–6
### Playing by the Rules

Jews weren't allowed to charge interest when they loaned money to fellow Jews—but many of them did anyway. That, combined with a drought, caused poor Jews to go deeply in debt. Some of their children were even forced into slavery as payment. Unscrupulous business practices continue to this day, with desperate people being forced to take "payday loans" with interest rates so high that they're illegal. If you loan money to someone, it's reasonable to expect to be repaid, but be considerate and don't press them for prompt repayment if they're unable.

# NEHEMIAH 7
## Keeping Careful Records

A priest once married a daughter of Barzillai and took on Barzillai's family name in the process. This somehow mixed up his family records, and his sons then couldn't prove they were Levites. So they were excluded from the priesthood (Nehemiah 7:63–65). Have you ever ended up in a quandary because of a technical error—whether due to carelessness or a misunderstanding? It can be extremely frustrating and time-consuming to get it all sorted out. Trust God to give you the wisdom to eventually fix things, and be prepared to learn patience.

## Don't Weep—God Loves You

The Feast of Booths was meant to be a happy harvest festival (Leviticus 23:37–40), but the Jews were weeping as they heard the scriptures being read. So Nehemiah told them not to grieve, for the joy of the Lord was their strength (Nehemiah 8:10). It's right to mourn if you've sinned and need to repent (James 4:8–10), but unfortunately, many Christians repent then *continue* repenting again and again, beating themselves up and living condemned by past sins. Take heart! God has forgiven you. You need to accept His forgiveness and forgive yourself.

## The Difficult Short List

After confessing that they and their ancestors had disobeyed God, the Jews promised to obey His Law and deliberately listed several laws which they were constantly being challenged to obey (Nehemiah 10:30–39). They knew if they could just live this "short list," they could manage the rest. Perhaps you'd find it beneficial to make a short list of *your* greatest challenges as a Christian. For example: "God, please help me to bless and speak well of all people, to love my enemies, to not hold grudges, to be slow to anger, to be honest in business, etc."

........................................................................................

........................................................................................

........................................................................................

........................................................................................

........................................................................................

........................................................................................

........................................................................................

........................................................................................

........................................................................................

## Volunteers for Jerusalem

Most of Jerusalem was still a postwar disaster zone—just heaps of rubble from destroyed houses (Nehemiah 2:17). So the Jews cast lots (rolled the dice) to determine who should move out of their country homes into this mess. Some Jews actually volunteered (11:1–2). Have you ever been forced to downsize, to move out of a nice, modern home in the suburbs into a rundown house in a rough neighborhood? Now imagine volunteering to do that—say, for example, going as missionaries to a Third World country. That takes real faith and unselfishness.

## Stop the Enemy's Inroads

———◦◦◦———

No Ammonite was to be allowed in the assembly, yet a priest who was close friends with Tobiah the Ammonite gave him use of a large storeroom inside the temple. With no room to store food for the priests, they were forced to stop work in the temple and go home. Things can quickly get to a sad state when you start to compromise with the godless. It often begins when you owe them favors for things they've done for you, so you bend the rules to please them. *Don't.* Such compromise can greatly hinder God's work.

# ESTHER

Esther, the cousin of Mordecai, becomes Queen of Persia without revealing her Jewish heritage. An official named Haman, angered by Mordecai's refusal to bow to him, plots to kill every Jew in the Persian Empire. Mordecai asks Esther to use her position as queen to rescue her people, but the Persians have a rule that anyone who enters the king's presence unbidden must be killed. So Esther risks her life to enter the throne room and request protection for her people. The king has Haman executed and the Jews prevail. They commemorate the event with a holiday called Purim.

## ESTHER 1–2
### God's Mysterious Ways

Often you may fail to see signs of God at work in your workplace or in your circle of family and friends—or in breaking news. You may have difficulty believing that God is involved in the messy, problem-filled lives of humans today. But look how He worked in a Persian monarch's drunken party, the proud refusal of a queen, and the events that followed. Undetected, the God who guides the nations was molding events to seat a beautiful young Jewess on the throne of Persia. God is still active in the world and in your life today.

## ESTHER 3–5
### Plots of the Wicked

---

Just as God is working to bring about His will, the devil is constantly striving to frustrate God's plans. He had the Persian king promote Haman the Agagite (a bitter enemy of Jews) to a position of great power. Soon Haman was plotting to exterminate the Jews. Sometimes you too will face huge problems, and it may appear that God is absent from the scene while the devil is having his way, unrestrained. But know this: God has a still higher plan, one that will ultimately defeat all the machinations of the evil one and bring about good (Romans 8:28).

## ESTHER 6–8
### Completely Changing Situations

———◦◦◦———

Just when things looked most hopeless for the Jews—and for Mordecai personally—God initiated the next phase of His plan by making the king sleepless one night. Mordecai and Esther had to do what *they* could do, true, but God was also working mightily to change circumstances. When you face trouble and/or danger, the Lord requires you to have courage and take action, but don't get the idea that you must overcome trouble alone. You'll only emerge victorious if God is working behind the scenes—or out in the open—on your behalf.

## ESTHER 9–10
### Remembering God's Goodness

———•◦•———

Over time, people tend to forget the miracles God has done. To be sure, they're overjoyed at the time when great danger misses them by a hair's breadth, but after a while, the humdrum of daily life begins to mute even vivid memories. That's why the Jews decided to celebrate Purim every year—to remind them that God had protected them in His great love for them. Do you annually celebrate His great deeds in *your* life? You celebrate your birthday and your wedding anniversary, but are there other amazing days you ought to be commemorating?

# JOB

Job is a wealthy, righteous farmer from the land of
Uz (1:1). The devil asks for God's permission to
attack Job's possessions then wipes out his livestock
and his children. But Job keeps his faith. Satan then
receives God's permission to attack Job's health. Job
then begins to question why God would allow him
to suffer so much. Then his four friends accuse him
of secretly sinning. In the end, God Himself speaks.
God asks questions that show His vast knowledge—
implying that Job should simply trust Him. He then
restores Job's health, possessions, and family.

## JOB 1–3
### Behind the Scenes

———•◆•———

Imagine how mysterious this book would be if it were missing the behind-the-scenes explanation of the first two chapters. This explanation draws the curtains aside and lets you understand why God allowed Job to suffer so greatly. It was received by revelation sometime *after* the events in this book were written. But God doesn't always give you clear insight into what's happening in your life. Often you can make neither heads nor tails out of why you're experiencing trouble. But the book of Job teaches you to keep trusting God. He knows that's asking a lot, but He asks anyway.

................................................................

................................................................

................................................................

................................................................

................................................................

................................................................

................................................................

................................................................

................................................................

## Simplistic Explanations

Job's friends came to comfort him, but they were soon taking it upon themselves to explain why God was permitting him to experience trouble. They had doctrines to explain everything, and the default answer in this case was that God was punishing Job for sin. As they reminded him, those who plow evil and those who sow trouble reap it (Job 4:8). So they urged Job to confess. Avoid shoving "default solutions" on people, or applying simplistic explanations like Band-Aids to deep wounds. The people around you need the benefit of the doubt and compassion not judgment.

......................................................................................

......................................................................................

......................................................................................

......................................................................................

......................................................................................

......................................................................................

......................................................................................

......................................................................................

......................................................................................

......................................................................................

## If You're Upright. . .

Bildad insisted that God had killed Job's children because they'd sinned. However, he said that if righteous Job sought God, He would swiftly restore *his* fortunes (Job 8:4–6). Bildad believed that though God might let the righteous suffer, it wouldn't be for long, then He would quickly end their woes and make them joyful again (vv. 20–21). Many modern Christians have this view. This outlook allows that the righteous may briefly experience suffering, but it puts pressure on people to quickly recover to *prove* they're righteous. This also is a simplistic explanation.

## But I'm Innocent!

———— ·◈· ————

Zophar conceded that Job was generally righteous but still thought Job had sinned, so he urged him to get right with God, and God would restore Job's fortunes. Then Job would once again rest securely and be blessed (Job 11:13–19). Job acknowledged that this doctrine was generally true and asked who didn't know these things (12:3). But this outlook isn't the complete answer to "Why suffering?" either. Like these men, your friends may also run through the whole litany of explanations as to why God allows you to suffer. Try not to subject others to this.

## JOB 13–15
### Silence Is Golden

———— ◆ ————

Job told his friends that although they thought they were so smart, he also had a brain and knew these things. He called them worthless physicians who couldn't correctly diagnose the problem and told them the smartest thing they could do was be quiet (Job 13:4–5). Too many believers feel compelled to tell people things they already know. Like blindfolded children playing pin the tail on the donkey, this usually involves blindly fixing the blame not the problem. Often the best thing you can do is sit quietly with a sufferer and just be there for them.

## Speak Encouraging Words

Job told his friends that if their roles were reversed, he could also give canned answers like they were doing. He could wax eloquent and show off his Bible knowledge, oblivious to the fact that they were suffering. But he said he'd encourage and comfort them instead (Job 16:4–5). Have compassion on those who are hurting. Show them love and concern. Even if your explanation of why they're suffering is technically correct, they'll benefit more from someone who *doesn't* have it all figured out, but who has a listening ear and offers words of comfort.

## Hurling Accusations

Job kept insisting that he was innocent and hadn't sinned, and that as far as he could see, God had afflicted him without cause. This caused a man named Zophar to completely lose it. He started hurling vicious, unsubstantiated accusations at Job, hoping some of them would stick (Job 22:5–11). This, unfortunately, is often the sad endgame when you begin blaming others. If they continue to insist they're innocent, you might drop all pretense of caring and angrily give them both barrels—to "defend God's reputation" of course. Please avoid this like the plague.

## Chastisement—Not Wrath

Zophar's speech wasn't *all* hot air. He made one very insightful observation—so good that it's basically the heart of the book of Job. He said that when God had tested him, he would come forth as gold (Job 23:10). Gold is melted down in a furnace and silver in a crucible, because it's only then that impurities can be skimmed off (Proverbs 17:3). Jesus said that He rebukes and chastises those He loves, so you are to be zealous and repent (Revelation 3:19). He only puts you through fiery trials and tests to purify you.

## Job's Expectations

Life hadn't turned out the way Job had expected. . .*at all*. He'd expected to live a long, full life being prosperous and in good health till the end, with God's blessing always upon him and all men praising him (Job 29:18–20). But though he had hoped for these things, evil had come instead (30:26). From reading the first two chapters, you understand why, but the thing is, when suffering happens to you, frequently life suddenly makes *no* sense. It's one thing to read about suffering. It's quite another to experience it.

## The Patience of Elihu

A young man named Elihu had waited his turn to speak, and now he became angry with Job for insisting that he didn't deserve how God had treated him instead of affirming God's goodness. In the end, God rebuked Job's other three friends for their words but *not* Elihu (Job 42:7–9) because Elihu was right. Elihu showed great restraint in waiting so long before speaking. This is an uncommon virtue these days. Don't rush in to give your opinion. Chances are good you'll be wrong anyway. James advises believers to be slow to speak (James 1:19).

## Job's Faults

It wasn't some sin in Job's life that had caused his troubles, but the things he said when enduring his troubles revealed flaws in his attitude anyway. As Elihu pointed out, Job was saying that he was innocent, but God had denied him justice, and was basically insinuating that he was more righteous than God (Job 34:5, 9; 35:2). Like Job, you may have a tendency to justify yourself, and that's understandable. But take care that you don't paint a picture of God being unrighteous or unfair and of yourself as righteous and innocent, deserving of better treatment from Him.

...........................................................................................

...........................................................................................

...........................................................................................

...........................................................................................

...........................................................................................

...........................................................................................

...........................................................................................

...........................................................................................

...........................................................................................

...........................................................................................

# God Speaks to Job

When God appeared in a windstorm, He didn't explain that Satan had asked permission to put Job to the test. (He revealed that later.) Instead, He asked Job a series of questions that showed that His wisdom was far superior to Job's. It was intended to help Job realize how little he knew of *any* of God's doings. In Isaiah 55:8–9, God states that His ways are much higher than your ways. You can't understand all God's ways of dealing with you. That's why you must simply place your hand in His and trust Him.

## God's Awesome Wisdom

———◆———

God asked Job how he could question His wisdom when he was ignorant even of how God operated in nature (Job 42:3). Job admitted
that he had talked about things he didn't understand. You will often
be in a similar situation. You may get a glimpse of God's hidden plans
but still not understand them. They would resemble immense screens
of incomprehensible code scrolling down. You couldn't even begin
to understand what they meant. You wouldn't know whether they
were immensely complex or just a meaningless jumble of numbers
and symbols. Welcome to God's super-complex wisdom.

.............................................................................................................

.............................................................................................................

.............................................................................................................

.............................................................................................................

.............................................................................................................

.............................................................................................................

.............................................................................................................

.............................................................................................................

.............................................................................................................

.............................................................................................................

# PSALMS

Over several centuries, God led various individuals to compose songs and poems of which 150 were later compiled into the book of Psalms. Many psalms, but not all, were written by David. Highlights of the book include Psalm 23; David's cry for forgiveness after his sin with Bathsheba (51); psalms of praise (100); and the celebration of scripture found in Psalm 119. Some psalms, called "imprecatory," call for God's judgment on enemies (see Psalms 69 and 109). Many psalms express agony of spirit, but nearly every psalm returns to the theme of praise to God.

# PSALMS 1–7
## God, Fight for Me!

Many of the psalms were written by David, a powerful fighter who waged war against multitudes of enemies. He cried out in strong prayers asking God to arise in anger, to defend him from the rage of his enemies (Psalm 7:6). Like David, you may often find yourself in desperate situations, outgunned and outnumbered. It may look like you're about to be overwhelmed. But you shouldn't depend on your own might to win. Your enemies may be angry, but you must trust that God will get angry *too*—and fight for you.

## When God Seems Distant

————— •◦• —————

David and the other psalmists expressed their emotions honestly, saying things you might hesitate to say. For example, in Psalm 10:1, David asks the Lord why He stands far off or why He hides Himself when he's in trouble. It might seem disrespectful to practically accuse God of standing to the side watching you go down but doing nothing to help or of hiding from you when you're in trouble and desperately need Him. But God sees your heart. He knows the difference between an anguished cry and an accusation. Pray honest but respectful prayers.

## PSALMS 15–18
### You're All I Have

———— ••• ————

Moses commanded the Israelites to love God with all their heart, strength, and soul, and it's clear from David's psalms that he loved God passionately. In Psalm 16:2 he states that God is his Lord and apart from Him, David had nothing. As king, David possessed wealth, women, and wine, yet he said in Psalm 63:1 that his soul thirsted for God and longed for Him in a dry and thirsty, waterless land. Like David, may you find ultimate fulfillment in the Lord not the things of earth. May you find meaning and purpose in the eternal God.

# PSALMS 19–23
## God's Hidden Messages

God has concealed many prophetic messages within the Psalms. For example, David gave voice to his emotions, asking, "My God, my God, why have You forsaken me?" (Psalm 22:1), and Israel's Messiah would later echo these words (Mark 15:34) and fulfill many of the following prophecies in this psalm (see Psalm 22:7–8, 14–18). Learn to tune in to God's hidden messages to *you*, speaking directly to you from a familiar Bible story, tugging at your heartstrings through a song, hiding in plain sight in the remarks of a friend, or shouting out to you in a glorious sunset.

## PSALMS 24–29
### The Beauty of the Lord

In Psalm 27:4, David wrote that the only thing he desired was to seek the Lord in His sanctuary and to gaze upon His breathtaking beauty. We aren't told when, but apparently David *had* experienced just such a holy encounter (Psalm 63:1–2), and it had left him longing for more. You may never have felt God palpably present, but have you ever sensed the presence of His Spirit however briefly or faintly? Think about it for a moment. God still requires you to follow Him by faith, but it's wonderful when He gives you a passing glimpse of His beauty.

## Your Sins Are Forgiven

---

A recurrent theme in the Bible is this: if God's people repent, He forgives their sins. David declared that he'd confess his transgressions to the Lord because every time he'd done it in the past, God had forgiven him and removed his guilt (Psalm 32:5). Have you repented of some sin and determined to walk close to the Lord again? Then cheer up! Stop beating yourself up. God has forgiven you (Isaiah 1:18; 1 John 1:7–9). Even if you stumble once again, repent again, commit yourself anew into God's hands, and walk in His grace once more.

It pays to be cautious, as that keeps you from recklessly exposing yourself to danger. But God doesn't want His children to be paralyzed by fear, afraid of enemies, or anxious about stepping out into His will. David was afraid when the Philistines seized him in Gath, but he sought the Lord, who then delivered him from all his fears (Psalm 34:4). Like David, you are to fear God more than any man because He can not only deliver you from the dangerous circumstances you fear, but set you free from the grip of fearful emotions.

## PSALMS 37–39
### Delighting in God

—•◦•—

God often delights to let you enjoy comfort, abundance, and pleasure. However, just as frequently, He knows it's best to withhold from you what are normally perfectly legitimate desires. You may be in a season of pruning, when God delights in paring from your life anything that distracts you from vital spiritual growth. David said that if you delight yourself in the Lord—and this includes delighting in His difficult will—He will give you what you desire (Psalm 37:4). So make up your mind to desire the things *God* wants for your life and then accept what He gives you.

## PSALMS 40–44
### *Waiting Patiently for God*

———•◦•———

While God may call on you to accept hardship and lack for an extended period of time, it's not His will that you put up with hazardous, immoral, or spiritually unhealthy situations. God promises to rescue you from these. David said that he waited patiently for the Lord, and though it took a while, God eventually answered him (Psalm 40:1–2). Because His love is unfailing, you can be certain that God will stir to action and rescue you as well (44:26). You need to pray then wait patiently while He's answering your prayers.

...................................................................

...................................................................

...................................................................

...................................................................

...................................................................

...................................................................

...................................................................

...................................................................

...................................................................

...................................................................

...................................................................

# PSALMS 45–49
## Troubled Times

---

When you experience unrelenting troubles and hardships, it's easy to get the impression that though God promised to never leave you that He *has*, in fact, forsaken you. Desperate, you think of a hundred things you've done that might have displeased Him. You even consider forgiven past sins. What you *ought* to do, however, is remind yourself that God is your refuge, an ever-present help in trouble (Psalm 46:1). He is *ever*-present. He is always there, watching over you. He hasn't even blinked. Though you have many troubles, He will deliver you (34:19).

## PSALMS 50–54
### Prayer of Repentance

King David wholeheartedly repented of committing adultery with Bathsheba and of orchestrating her husband's death. In Psalm 51, David admitted his guilt. But while it's not surprising that he believed God would forgive him, what *is* surprising are his repeated requests for God to swiftly restore *joy* to him (vv. 8, 12). Many Christians believe that they must flagellate themselves a long time before God is satisfied and begrudgingly forgives them—let alone that He would have any desire to bring joy into their lives. But as Psalm 34:18 says, God draws near to contrite, brokenhearted sinners.

## PSALMS 55–59
### Giving Your Cares to God

Psalm 55:22 tells you to cast your cares on the Lord, being convinced that He can hold you up and take care of you. But the problem may be that although you believe the Lord is *able* to sustain you, you're not sure that He's *inclined* to. You may often feel like a failure, certain that God is fed up with you. That's where 1 Peter 5:7 comes in. It echoes Psalm 55:22 but adds a new wrinkle, telling you to cast all your care upon God, being assured that He loves and cares for you.

## PSALMS 60–65
### Never Stop Trusting

————·◦·————

There will be times when God allows you to experience a great deal of frustration, or pain, or anxiety, and you may wonder if He's in control of things, or whether the entire world has run amok. It can be difficult to love Him at times like that. Instead of being your refuge from the storm, it can seem that God is the one *causing* the storm. But Psalm 62:8 urges you to trust in the Lord at *all* times and pour out your heart to Him, for He *is* your refuge. Never stop trusting Him.

........................................................................

........................................................................

........................................................................

........................................................................

........................................................................

........................................................................

........................................................................

........................................................................

........................................................................

........................................................................

........................................................................

........................................................................

........................................................................

........................................................................

## PSALMS 66–68
### The Lord Carries You

Psalm 68:19 instructs you to praise the Lord who bears your burdens day by day. The Bible pictures God as a mother eagle bearing her young aloft on great wings (Deuteronomy 32:10–11). Jesus said He was the good shepherd and described a shepherd joyfully carrying a lost lamb home on His shoulders (John 10:11; Luke 15:4–6). At times, you may feel you're enduring great problems all by yourself, but God has come down to take much of the weight on His shoulders. You are not forgotten, and you are not alone.

# PSALMS 69–71
## Sinking in Troubles

In Psalm 69:1–2 David prayed for God to save him because, as he described it, the waters had come up to his neck and he was sinking in miry depths where there was no foothold. (See also vv. 14–15.) You may feel that desperate at times. You're overwhelmed, not even sure that you're going to make it (see Psalm 77). But no matter how hopeless things looked, David knew where he could turn to for help—and this help is still available to you today. God is the hope of the hopeless.

## PSALMS 72–75
### Longing for Riches

In Psalm 73:2–3, a man named Asaph confessed that his feet had almost slipped off the path of godliness when he envied the prosperity of the wicked. It's normal to feel a twinge of longing when you think about how rich some people are while you're barely making it. But avoid setting your heart on acquiring wealth. People who covet riches fall into all kinds of temptations, and the selfish path to wealth injures their souls (1 Timothy 6:9). While it's good to earn a decent living, longing to be rich has built-in pitfalls.

## God Is Light

Psalm 84:11 states that the Lord is both a sun and a shield. He is both light and an impenetrable force field. An unknown psalmist declared that God is radiant with light (76:4), and that those who walk in the light of His presence are truly blessed (89:15). The Bible constantly describes God as light and as dwelling in light. It promises you that if you live in the light as He is in the light, you will have perfect communion with Him, and the blood of Jesus will cleanse you from all sin (1 John 1:7).

## Desperate Times

You can be sailing along with everything beautifully calm, and suddenly a storm of life can sweep over the horizon, plunging your world into chaos. In times like this, Psalm 79:8 is particularly relevant because it reminds God you have dire need and implores Him to quickly help you. The apostle Paul knew what it was like to be desperate. He was sometimes under great pressure, far beyond his ability to endure, so that he despaired of life itself (2 Corinthians 1:8). That's when it's so good to know that God is on your side.

## PSALMS 82–87
### Abounding in Love

Psalm 86:5 declares that the Lord is forgiving and good, abounding in love to all who call on Him. Verse 15 states that God is a compassionate and gracious God, slow to anger, and abounding in love and faithfulness. When you're enduring prolonged discouragement, loss, oppression, or setbacks in your life, your health, or your finances, remember all the amazing attributes of God. They describe who He is, and who He is, is *so* good that it should impel you to reach out to Him in your time of need.

## PSALMS 88–90
### The Eternal God

God existed before there was a physical universe, before the stars formed or the first planet came into being. Psalm 90:2 tells you that even long before God brought forth the world, and before the tectonic forces caused the mountains to be born, God already existed. Knowing this informs you of how big and powerful the Lord is. It lets you know that He will always be around for you. He isn't going anywhere. And if you trust in a God that big and powerful, and who loves you more than you can imagine, you won't be moved either.

## Close to God

The Bible states that whoever dwells in the shelter of the Most High God will rest in complete peace in His shadow (Psalm 91:1). You can't see God. If you could, you'd be immediately convinced that He's able to protect you. But you *can* trust God's Word when it describes what a strong shelter He is. This trust will give you perfect peace. There are many dark and devious forces that threaten to undo you, and they never seem to stop trying to tear you down. But God has strong, protective arms around you and can keep you safe.

## PSALMS 97–102
### Worship Joyfully

Psalm 100:1–2 urges you to shout for joy to the Lord, to worship Him with gladness, and to come before Him with joyful songs. That's a big emphasis on joy and happiness, but you may wonder how to have it come into your life. Do you "fake it till you make it"—pretend that you're joyful until you really feel joy? No, but it helps to make a conscious decision to trust that God is good, loves you, and is working to bring good into your life. Believe that, and you'll begin to be happy.

---

Psalm 103:13–14 says that as a father has compassion on his children, so the Lord has compassion on you. He remembers that you're weak. He knows you're hardwired with self-preserving instincts, and though you have altruistic intentions, you don't always carry them out. This is not to excuse willful selfish choices, but it explains many of your failings. God knows that your spirit is willing, but your flesh is weak (Matthew 26:41), and takes this into account. He wants you to grow, but He knows the process will take time, so He is loving and patient.

## PSALMS 106–107
### Thanking the Lord

Think you only know about a few things God is doing in your life? He does many other things you're not even aware of. But as long as you believe that He loves you, you can *expect* Him to constantly be looking for ways to bless you and to make His love and grace overflow in your life. Psalm 107:31 tells you to give thanks to the Lord for His unfailing love and for His wonderful deeds for you. Thank Him for the things you're aware of, and for all that He does for you that goes unnoticed.

# PSALMS 108–113
## Hope Despite Despair

If God truly loves you, you'd expect Him to be looking out for you around the clock. You'd expect Him to always be watching your back and to set to work rescuing you when you fall. Psalm 112:4 says that light dawns for the upright even in obscure darkness. In other words, even when your life is mantled in Stygian darkness, you can count on God to faithfully send the light again. It won't stay dark, even though all seems lost in deep gloom now. The sun will shine again.

## Loving God in Return

In Psalm 116:1, the writer stated that he loved the Lord because He had heard him crying out for mercy. This is echoed in 1 John 4:19, which states that Christians love God because He first loved them. This may sound selfish, but God designed you to appreciate and respond to His love. He's okay with you loving Him after you experience His love. Jesus once explained that a woman who had been forgiven for many sins responded to Him with great love (Luke 7:44–47). What good thing has God done for you? What was your response?

........................................................................................

........................................................................................

........................................................................................

........................................................................................

........................................................................................

........................................................................................

........................................................................................

........................................................................................

........................................................................................

........................................................................................

## God Is Good

Some Christians are fond of saying, "God is good. . .*all the time.*" Why are the three words tacked on the end? Because although the Bible repeatedly affirms that God is good, and we sense deep in our hearts that it must be true, there are times when it seems that what God does—or allows to happen—*isn't* good. But Psalm 119:68 succinctly says that God *is* good and what He *does* is good. The problem is that we, as limited mortals, are unable to see the big picture, and won't until we enter eternity.

## The Lord's Help

When you're going through a crisis—say you're being attacked by enemies—and God does a miracle to rescue you, you're very aware of His help. But after a while, you can forget what He's done. You might even begin to think that you handled the emergency on your own. So it pays to remember, as Psalm 124:2–3 says, that if the Lord had not been on your side when they attacked you, they would have swallowed you alive. God is the only One standing between you and disaster. Always remember that.

.......................................................................................................

.......................................................................................................

.......................................................................................................

.......................................................................................................

.......................................................................................................

.......................................................................................................

.......................................................................................................

.......................................................................................................

.......................................................................................................

.......................................................................................................

## PSALMS 126–135
*Cloudbursts of Blessing*

---

The Negev is the arid land in the south of Israel. It mainly rains in winter, and when it does, its deep, bone-dry ravines fill with rushing water—and the land returns to life. This is what the psalmist meant when he asked God to restore his fortunes like streams in the Negev (Psalm 126:4). Sometimes you go through dry seasons in your life when the heavens seem like unrelenting brass overhead, and God withholds His rain. But know this: refreshment will come again. In due season God's blessing will return—just like water returns to streams in the Negev.

## PSALMS 136–140
### God Knows You

———※———

David was aware that the Lord had searched his heart and knew him thoroughly (Psalm 139:1). God knew David down to the tiniest molecules of his DNA. He knew every memory cell in David's brain. He knew how David would react in any given situation. And God knows you inside and out as well. He designed David for a specific purpose, and He has designed you for a unique mission in life as well. The God who knows you completely has prepared a path for your feet. He knows you inside out.

## PSALMS 141–144; PSALM 145:1–9
### When You're Weak

———••••———

An unknown psalmist wrote that even when his spirit grew faint and weak, God continued watching over him (Psalm 142:3). Even if you've been struggling for a long time and have become weary and discouraged, don't stop trusting that God is guarding you. When you're too tired to persevere, God is still able to bless you, to uphold you, and to cause you to succeed. Even if your feet stumble, He can pick you up. Psalm 145:14 agrees, saying that the Lord upholds all that fall and raises up all those who are bowed down.

## Praise the Lord

The book of Psalms ends with a resounding, joyful shout. Psalm 150:6 declares that everything that has breath should praise the Lord. David and the other psalmists considered praise to be an integral part of worshipping God. Praising God has a wonderful effect on you as well. It creates an awareness in you of how great He is and how He's able to answer your prayers. It ingrains a habit of thankfulness in you, which is essential for your spiritual health. And, very importantly, it brings you into union with God.

# PROVERBS

Proverbs doesn't have a story line—it's simply a collection of general precepts and practical tips for living. They are mainly from the pen of King Solomon, the wisest human being ever. In 1 Kings 3:12 God says that He gave Solomon a wise and an understanding heart, making him wiser than any other man had been. The proverbs speak about issues such as work, money, sex, temptation, drinking, laziness, discipline, and child rearing. Underlying each proverb is the truth that to revere the Lord is to begin to have true knowledge.

# PROVERBS 1–3
## The Beginning of Knowledge

You may be familiar with the phrase that declares that the fear of the Lord is the beginning of knowledge (Proverbs 1:7), but do you understand it? To fear God is to respect Him, to be in awe of Him, to be afraid to disobey Him. It means to be aware that you can't measure up to His standard of righteousness, and therefore deserve punishment, but that God chose to save you because of His great love. When you have such respect for God, you've laid the first brick in your foundation of true knowledge.

## PROVERBS 4–6
### Walking in Greater Light

In Proverbs 4:18 Solomon declares that the path of the righteous is like the morning sun, shining ever brighter until the full light of day. You can expect to get closer to God the more years you follow Him, as more of His truth and love are revealed to you. You may experience career setbacks, endure infirmities, and face financial problems that make it seem like things are getting *worse*. But this proverb remains true, despite life's difficulties. Though your outer physical body is perishing, your spirit is being renewed day by day (2 Corinthians 4:16).

# PROVERBS 7–9
## Hate Pride and Evil

———•◦•———

Proverbs 8:13 gives clear, basic reasons why you should fear God. It states that to fear the Lord is to hate evil, pride, arrogance, evil behavior, and perverse speech. God hates these things, and disciples of Christ who strive to please their Lord must hate them too. You shouldn't want any of these things in your life, because God will punish whoever entertains them. The best way to guard yourself from these vices is to despise them and ruthlessly weed them from your heart whenever you find them popping up.

...........................................................................................................

...........................................................................................................

...........................................................................................................

...........................................................................................................

...........................................................................................................

...........................................................................................................

...........................................................................................................

...........................................................................................................

...........................................................................................................

...........................................................................................................

# PROVERBS 10–12
## Diligence versus Laziness

One of several recurring themes in the book of Proverbs is this: laziness results in poverty, but diligent work brings wealth (Proverbs 10:4). Of course, God isn't promising you fabulous riches. How *much* wealth it brings is relative. Many people work hard but never break out of the lower middle class. Also, unforeseen misfortunes can drain even hard-earned finances. Nevertheless, the general principle behind this proverb remains true. There will be ups and downs throughout the years, but your work ethic and habits, followed consistently over a lifetime, will bear this principle out.

## PROVERBS 13–15

### Integrity

Proverbs speaks a lot about integrity. To have integrity means to be honest and be guided by good moral principles. It means to be upright, honorable, and to have good character. Proverbs 13:6 and 11:3 say that the integrity of the upright guides them—helps them make good decisions—but that the deceitful are destroyed by their lying and double-dealing. Are you a man or woman of integrity? If so, God will put His Spirit and His blessing on your life, rescue you from trouble when it comes, and give you a good reputation.

## PROVERBS 16–18
### Committing Works to God

Proverbs 16:3 promises that if you commit what you do to the Lord, He will establish your plans. Whatever you're doing, lay your plans on God's altar, and ask Him to bless them and help you to accomplish them—*if* they're His will. You must also give the Lord free rein to alter them as He pleases. After all, He knows what will work. And you wouldn't want to succeed in an endeavor that dishonors Him, would you? Make God your partner—your senior partner with full veto privileges—in all that you do.

## Helping the Poor

God's Word constantly admonishes you to show consideration for the poor, telling you, if you're able, to loan money to the needy. Proverbs 19:17 states that if you show such kindness to the poor, you're actually lending money to the Lord, and He will repay you. If the thought of loaning a hundred dollars to the One who created the Milky Way galaxy sounds odd, remember that Jesus said that whatever good you do for a brother or sister in Christ, you're doing it to Him (Matthew 25:40). Of course, you should give wisely and within your means, but give.

## PROVERBS 22–23; PROVERBS 24:1–10
### Avoid Covetousness

————•◦•————

If you come up with clever business plans, seize golden opportunities, and are willing to put in long hours, you stand a chance of becoming wealthy. But beware if your entire goal is to become rich. Not only is covetousness detrimental to your spiritual health but to your physical and mental health as well. You're likely to crash and burn. Proverbs 23:4–5 bluntly advises you not to wear yourself out trying to gain riches. Thieves and economic downturns can wipe out years of hard work, so store your main treasures in heaven (Matthew 6:19–20).

## Thou Shalt Not Gloat

—·◆·—

Proverbs 24:17–18 commands you not to gloat when your enemy falls. If you do, it will displease God so much that He will stop judging them. Don't even judge people in your thoughts. This might be difficult for you. After all, if you hate someone, curse them, and pray for God to judge them, it's only natural to rejoice when He *does* judge them. But you're not to curse people either. Jesus said to pray for God to bless your enemies. If they're doing evil, well, pray that God blesses them with sincere repentance.

.................................................................................

.................................................................................

.................................................................................

.................................................................................

.................................................................................

.................................................................................

.................................................................................

.................................................................................

.................................................................................

.................................................................................

## PROVERBS 27–29
### Loving Rebukes

———————

You probably don't like getting rebuked and told that what you're doing is wrong. But if the person rebuking you is a true friend, someone whom you know has your best interests in mind, you can accept it and even be thankful. As Proverbs 27:5–6 says, you can trust a friend even if their words wound you. It's better that they confront you rather than say nothing. How well do you receive rebukes from a friend or family member? Do you have the courage to address an issue in a friend's life?

## PROVERBS 30–31

### Appreciation

———•✦•———

It's important to show appreciation when someone does good, especially if they make a lifetime habit of doing so. Proverbs 31 speaks of the virtues of a good wife, and verse 31 commands husbands to speak up and honor them for all that they do and to let everyone know that they appreciate them. In fact, everyone needs to be appreciated—husbands, wives, children, coworkers, etc. The Lord Himself commends people, saying, "Well done, good and faithful servant" (Matthew 25:21). Sincere praise and appreciation strengthen your spirit and your resolve.

# ECCLESIASTES

A king (commonly believed to be Solomon) pursues the things of this world, only to find them unfulfilling. Learning, pleasure, work, laughter—all are vanity and about as profitable as chasing after the wind (Ecclesiastes 1:2, 14). The king also laments the inequities of life: people live, work hard, and die, only to leave their belongings to someone else; the wicked frequently prosper more than—and rule over—the righteous; the poor are oppressed. Nevertheless, the king realizes that the bottom line is for people to fear God and keep His commandments. This is the entire duty of mankind (12:13).

## ECCLESIASTES 1–2; ECCLESIASTES 3:1–11
### A Meaningless Life

———◦◦◦———

As king of Israel, Solomon had experienced pretty much all that life had to offer, and he came to the conclusion that having great riches wasn't all it was chalked up to be. Living without God and only for one's self is a life without meaning. Whereas, if you *have* God in your life, you can find satisfaction in simple activities like eating and drinking and being fulfilled in your work (see Ecclesiastes 2:24). It's important also to do good to others. These basic things will bring you much happiness (3:12). This is true abundant life (John 10:10).

## Grasping for the Wind

---

Solomon observed that many "successful" people's lives were actually vain and useless. They thought they were so wise clutching solid, enduring material things, finding security and fulfillment in life's pleasures. But in reality, they were merely grasping at the wind. When it comes time to leave this fleeting life, they can take none of their material things with them. So what do they gain out of all their years of toil? Nothing. They merely frustrate themselves (see Ecclesiastes 5:15–17), because by living in the fast lane, they miss out on most of life's true pleasures.

## Appreciating Life

Solomon observed that it isn't wise to ask questions such as "Why were olden days better than life today?" (Ecclesiastes 7:10). Why? Because questions like that betray a deep dissatisfaction with your life. God tells you to be content with such things as you have because He—the source of true life—has promised to never leave you or forsake you (Hebrews 13:5). You may presently lack some things you used to have, you may not be as healthy as you once were, but these are not reasons to be ungrateful. Learn to be content with your life.

## ECCLESIASTES 9:11–18;
## ECCLESIASTES 10–12
### Simple Life Rules

———— • ◦ • ————

Much of Ecclesiastes presents life as a bleak, futile endeavor. And this is true for a life lived without God—and even for a believer if he or she expresses faith in God but doesn't keep Him as their center. In Ecclesiastes 12:13, Solomon states the conclusion of the matter: you are to fear God and keep His commandments if you wish to live a blessed, fulfilling life. And once you fear God and obey Him, and He blesses you, you'll have more reason to love Him. Do this and you're fulfilling the greatest command in the Law (Deuteronomy 6:5).

# SONG OF SOLOMON

A dark-skinned beauty is marrying the king, and both she and the king are thrilled. He tells her how beautiful she is in his eyes and compares the various parts of her anatomy to doves, a flock of sheep, a stately tower, and a royal garden of delights. She responds by telling him how handsome he is and how much she longs for him. Through eight chapters and 117 verses, the two lovers admire each other's physical beauty, expressing intense romantic love and devotion. Many Christians see this book as a metaphor for Christ and His Church.

In this passionate poem, the Song of Solomon, the woman says that her beloved is hers and she is his (Song of Solomon 2:16). He is hers and *only* hers, and she is his and *only* his. This speaks of an exclusive relationship. There is a similar refrain in Proverbs 5:15–19, where young men are told to drink deeply of their own well, and warned to let them be theirs *only*, and not to share this water with strangers. They are to forever rejoice in intimate pleasures with their own wife and be ravished with her love alone.

## Intimate Pleasures

———— • ✦ • ————

In Song of Solomon 7:6, the man exclaims how beautiful his wife is and what surpassing pleasure she gives him. He then describes her lovely body in poetic language. This is passionate, romantic love at its best, with a husband and wife enjoying the raptures of physical union, holy and unashamed. Many people forget that God was the one who created intimacy and who designed humans to desire it. The first command to appear in the Bible was not to love God or even to love your fellow man but to engage in physical intimacy (Genesis 1:28).

# ISAIAH

Like most prophets, Isaiah announces the bad news
of punishment for sin. But he also describes a coming
Messiah who will be wounded for humanity's sins
(Isaiah 53). Called to be a prophet through a vision
of God (chapter 6), Isaiah wrote a book that some call
"the fifth Gospel" for its many predictions of the birth,
life, and death of Jesus Christ. These prophecies of
redemption balance the threats of God's discipline
against Judah and Jerusalem. Isaiah's prophecies end
with chapters 40–66 describing God's restoration
of Israel, His promised salvation, and His eternal
kingdom.

## Undesired Blood Sacrifices

--------⊷◆⊶--------

Leviticus describes the proper way to perform animal sacrifices in great detail. But in Isaiah's day, God exclaimed that He'd had more than enough of burnt offerings and took no pleasure in the blood of bulls, lambs, and goats (Isaiah 1:11). Why? Because His people were only going through the motions. Their hearts were far from Him. Now, however, since Jesus shed His blood on the cross, God no longer desires animal sacrifices—even if properly performed on Mount Moriah—but seeks people to worship Him in Spirit and truth (John 4:21–24).

## ISAIAH 3–5
### The Lord's Vineyard

In this beautiful passage, God described the Israelites as a vineyard (Isaiah 5:1–7). Also, in Psalm 80:8–15, God described them as a choice vine He had brought out of Egypt. He planted it on a hill, and it sent its roots deep and soon grew great branches. But its grapes were very sour. God does everything He can to help you bear good fruit (Isaiah 5:4), but you have to be firmly connected to Him before that will happen. If you aren't in tune with Him, it's like you're bearing withered, tasteless grapes (John 15:4–6).

## ISAIAH 6–8
### Witnessing God's Message

In Isaiah 6:8, when Isaiah heard the Lord asking who He should send and who would go for Him, Isaiah answered that he was ready and willing. Many Christians think that the job of preaching the Gospel belongs to their pastor and to specially called missionaries. But *all* Christians are called to witness to others about Jesus (Mark 16:15). Are you reluctant or too timid to share God's message with the people around you? Then pray for God to give you more of His Spirit. It's the Spirit that gives you the power to witness (Acts 1:8).

## ISAIAH 9–10
### The Son of David

God had promised David that one of his sons would always sit on the throne of Israel (2 Samuel 7:16), and Isaiah 9:6–7 proclaims that one of David's descendants would also be called "Mighty God, Everlasting Father, Prince of Peace." How could a mere man be Mighty God? It's only possible because Jesus Christ, a descendant of David, is also the Son of God, God in the flesh. Never lose sight of how great and wonderful Jesus is. Knowing Him and longing to follow and obey Him has the power to transform your life.

.......................................................................................................................

.......................................................................................................................

.......................................................................................................................

.......................................................................................................................

.......................................................................................................................

.......................................................................................................................

.......................................................................................................................

.......................................................................................................................

.......................................................................................................................

.......................................................................................................................

# ISAIAH 11–13
## Christ's Millennial Kingdom

---

Isaiah 11:6 prophesies that one day the wolf will dwell peacefully with the lamb, and other once-savage beasts like lions and leopards will play with goats and calves. And little children will lead them. These amazing events will happen during the Millennium, the thousand-year kingdom of Christ on earth. And if you trust in Jesus to save you, you will be there in that day to enjoy an earth without war, an entire planet transformed into a paradise like the Garden of Eden. You'll have a glorified, powerful body, and you'll be literally immortal.

## ISAIAH 14–16
### Fallen from Heaven

———— • ◈ • ————

In Isaiah 14:4, the Lord describes the demise of the king of Babylon then goes deeper, relating the fall of the devil long ages ago (vv. 12–14), speaking of his lust for power and his desire to be like God. There are lessons for you here too. If you ever begin admiring your own beauty, intelligence, and talents, immediately humble yourself before God—or He will have to humble you. Or if God takes His time answering your prayers, and you begin to think you'd do a better job of running the world than He does, repent.

# Temple in Egypt

Isaiah 19:19 says that there would one day be an altar to the Lord in Egypt. There was a large Jewish population at Heliopolis, and about 200 BC, they built a temple then said that it "fulfilled prophecy." But they were merely rebelling against God's temple and priesthood in Jerusalem. People often search for scriptures that seem to condone something they want to do. Don't be misled. Peter warned Christians not to distort the Word of God to make it say something it doesn't actually say (2 Peter 3:16). Many people do this today. Don't follow them.

## Building in Vain

Isaiah 22:10 describes a king of Judah carefully preparing for an Assyrian siege, tearing down houses for stones to strengthen the city walls, and building a reservoir to store water inside the city. He gave much thought to practical details but failed to look to God. You are to give careful thought to all your plans, but it's even more important to seek the Lord. Without Him, you'll fail. A psalmist declared that unless the Lord builds the house, the builders labor in vain. Unless the Lord watches over the city, the guards watch in vain (Psalm 127:1).

---

The prophet declared that during troubled times, God is a refuge for the distressed and needy, a shelter from the tempest. The threats of the ruthless may be like a shrieking desert storm, clawing at your door, but God is a great stone wall protecting you (Isaiah 25:4). How often do you find this true? Even when you've failed to acknowledge your need for God during easy times, you can turn to Him and cry out for help when trouble strikes. And He has promised that if you wholeheartedly seek Him, you'll find Him (Jeremiah 29:13).

## ISAIAH 27–28
### Christ the Cornerstone

In Isaiah 28:16 the prophet declared that God had laid a stone in Zion, a precious cornerstone for a sure foundation, and that those who trust on it will never regret doing so. Peter explained that this prophecy refers to Christ (1 Peter 2:6). You are to build your life on the solid rock of Jesus' person and teachings (Ephesians 2:20). Make Him your foundation, rest securely on Him, and you won't be shaken or moved by life's disasters. Troubles and storms will come, of course, but you will endure (Matthew 7:24–25).

## Pretending to Love God

Isaiah prophesied that if you judged His people by their words, you'd think they were close to Him. And they seemed to honor Him. In reality, their hearts were far from Him (Isaiah 29:13). You may wonder if this describes you. Many Christians fret that they don't love God enough, that they are actually hypocrites, and that God therefore doesn't love them. Well, if your heart is far from God, you'll *know* it, but you'll try to cover it up. But if you sincerely desire to love God, you probably *do* love Him. You may just be too hard on yourself.

## ISAIAH 31–33
### Flesh versus Spirit

In Isaiah's day, the prophet reminded the Jews that the Egyptians were mere weak mortals and not God. Their horses were but flesh and not spirit (Isaiah 31:3). But even some believers worry that that's precisely the problem: God's powers are spiritual, and to them "spiritual" means invisible, barely there, and weak. You do well to be reminded that spiritual things are more valuable, more lasting, and far more powerful than the temporary physical things you can see and touch. Until you grasp that, you'll worry instead of being confident when required to trust God.

## ISAIAH 34–36
### God Will Rescue You

————◆◆◆————

You may often face discouragement and know other believers who struggle with sorrow and despair also. What should you do? Isaiah 35:3–4 tells you plainly: strengthen the feeble hands, steady the knees that are giving way, and encourage those with fearful hearts to be strong and not fear, because God will come to save them. Don't just give this counsel to others. Practice it yourself. Live it. Believe that God loves you, sees your plight, and is going to act. Then encourage others the same way that God has encouraged you (2 Corinthians 1:4).

## It Shall Not Be

In Isaiah 37:33 the prophet declared that the vast Assyrian army surrounding Jerusalem wouldn't enter the city or shoot an arrow in it. They wouldn't even build a siege ramp against it. Oftentimes your foes are a fearsome spectacle and demoralize you with their talk and bluster. But believe that God is with you, that their proud might will be shaken, and they'll be brought down. They may be so huge right now that they block the sunlight from reaching you, but God answers desperate prayers, and if He opposes them, they won't accomplish their purpose.

## Greater Than the Galaxies

---

In Isaiah 40:25 God asks who would you compare Him to or who is His equal? He then invites you to take your weary eyes off the problems surrounding you and to look up at the starry hosts. What powerful Being created all these? God did! And He calls all the hundreds of billions of stars by name. In fact, some of those stars you see are entire *galaxies*–the Andromeda galaxy in the northern hemisphere, and the Magellanic Clouds (Large and Small) in the south. Look up and be in awe of the Almighty!

## Messianic Prophecies

In Isaiah 42:6–7 God promised a mysterious "servant" whom He would appoint to be a light to the nations in order to open blind eyes, to bring out prisoners from the dungeon, and rescue those sitting in darkness from prison. Jesus proclaimed that He fulfilled this prophecy (Luke 4:18–19). Has Jesus set you free from prison? The life of God's suffering Servant, Jesus, was repeatedly foretold in Isaiah. The prophecies spoke of a compassionate, loving ruler who would soothe your sorrows and carry your burdens. Do you let Jesus do all this for you?

## ISAIAH 44–45
### *Unprofitable Deities*

In modern times, men and women still worship idols, only instead of statues of gold and silver, they put their trust in bank accounts, a dream house, shiny new cars, or their career. An idol can be anything that you love and put above God's will. But what you treasure so highly won't profit you in the day of trouble (see Isaiah 44:9; 46:7). Renounce anything in your life that's in danger of becoming an idol to you. Lay it on God's altar, trust wholly in Him, and let Him have His way with it.

## ISAIAH 46–48
### Useless Astrology

———◆———

Belief in astrology is widespread among the unsaved, and many people today plan major life decisions around astromancy (daily predictions). But in Isaiah 47:13, God challenged Babylonian astrologers to save them from the doom that was coming upon them. Stargazers made predictions month by month, but God warned that a catastrophe they couldn't foresee would destroy them. Astrology is based on the belief that distant gods (the planets) control events on earth. But the Lord is in control. He created the planets, distant orbs of rock and gas and ice, so put your trust in Him.

## ISAIAH 49–50
### God Will Reward You

————•◦•————

Israel said that they had labored in vain, they had exhausted their strength trying to serve God but had accomplished nothing. Nevertheless, they added that they trusted the Lord had seen their efforts and would reward them (Isaiah 49:4). God does see. And He does reward. Hebrews 6:10 assures you that God will not forget the love you have shown Him as you helped Him and His people. No work done in love is in vain. God will redeem all your broken efforts and see to it that you're rewarded for all you do.

# ISAIAH 51–53
## Prophecies of the Messiah

---

Isaiah 52:13–15 and 53:1–12 are some very powerful Messianic prophecies. They describe the trial, mockery, death, and burial of Israel's king in astonishing detail some six hundred years before these events happened. These scriptures also clearly explain that Jesus died to pay the price for your sins. These fulfilled prophecies should greatly increase your faith. Pray that God will open your eyes to wondrous things in His Word (Psalm 119:18), so you'll understand things you've never grasped before. Read these prophecies and thank God that He loved you enough to send Jesus.

## ISAIAH 54–56
### Compassion after Chastisement

———◦◦◦———

In Isaiah 54:7–8 God said that for a brief moment He had abandoned Israel, but with deep compassion He would gather them. In a surge of anger, He hid His face from them for a moment, but with everlasting kindness He would have compassion on them. What may seem to be a long dry season in your life—months or even years of chastisement—is, to God, but a short moment. Have hope! Hang in there. Twice in this passage God said He is moved with pity or compassion for His people. He hasn't forgotten you.

## ISAIAH 57–59
### Truly Obeying God

God told His people to hold an annual day of fasting (Leviticus 16:29–30) when He would atone for their sins. But the Jews missed the point of what that entailed. They went through the motions of fasting and mourning but failed to repent or change their ways. This can happen to you today too. God tells you to do something, so you go through the motions of obeying Him but may fail to act in love toward your fellow man. Don't miss the heart of Christ's message. Above all things, make sure you're motivated by love.

## God Brings Joy

God saw those who grieved in Zion, and He was determined to bestow on them a crown of beauty instead of a face smeared with ashes, the oil of joy instead of mourning, and a garment of praise instead of a spirit of despair (Isaiah 61:2–3). You can appropriate these promises as well. Are you mourning? God longs to wipe away the ashes, to crown you with His Spirit, to joyfully anoint your head with oil, remove your sackcloth, and clothe you in pure white linen, so that you may enter His presence and praise Him.

## He Knows Your Sorrow

In one of the shortest, most moving phrases in the Bible, Isaiah 63:9 tells you that in all His peoples' distress, God too was distressed. He knows exactly what you're feeling. He knows what you're going through. Hebrews 4:15 says that you have a high priest who is able to empathize with your weaknesses because He was also tempted in every way, just as you are. Whether you're distressed by hardship, temptation, or sickness, Jesus knows your feelings intimately. He feels distress when *you* feel distress. He's on the same page as you.

## Heaven on Earth

In Isaiah 66:22 God promised that the new heavens and the new earth that He will make will endure forever. This old world has a lot wrong with it, and one day, God is going to bring it to an end. In its place, God will create a new, transformed planet, made out of super physical-spiritual materials. That's why the new earth will endure forever. That's why God's gigantic, eternal city will be able to rest on the earth. That's why you, in your new, glorified, eternal body will be able to live on it forever.

# JEREMIAH

—◆◆◆—

Called to be a prophet as a youth (Jeremiah 1:6), Jeremiah prophesies bad news to Judah: the Lord is about to bring the overpowering armies of the distant nation of Babylon upon His idolatrous, disobedient people (5:15). Jeremiah, however, is mocked for his warnings, beaten, locked in stocks, and imprisoned in a muddy cistern (chapter 38). But his words come true with the Babylonian invasion of chapter 52. But God promises that following judgment, there will be days filled with blessings (24:4–7). In fact, the book of Jeremiah contains a wonderful prophecy about God's new covenant in Jesus (see 31:31–34).

# JEREMIAH 1–2
## Drinking Living Water

The Jews had forsaken God, the spring of living water, and had carved out cisterns (underground caverns) to store rainwater. Men applied a coat of plaster to cisterns so they wouldn't leak, but frequent earthquakes caused cracks to appear, and the water drained away (Jeremiah 2:13). Be satisfied with God, the source of eternal life, and don't seek to make up your own ineffective religion based on the way you reason God ought to think and behave. God knows what He's doing, and your attempts to create a homemade religion won't work.

## Truly Knowing God

God declared that His people had become foolish and didn't really know Him. They were senseless children who had no understanding (Jeremiah 4:22). The apostle John said that if you say you know God but hate your fellow man, you aren't telling the truth (1 John 4:7–8, 20–21). You can be wise according to the ways of this world, a literal genius, and have vast knowledge, but if you don't truly *know* God and obey His rules, then you've missed the point of life. Love God and your fellow man. Then you'll truly know Him.

## JEREMIAH 5–6
### Longing to Do You Good

God desires to do good things for you, but He can't do the good He wants to if you're disobeying Him. Your sins prevent His blessings from flowing into your life, and your disobediences repel good things (Jeremiah 5:25). What do you do if you pray daily for God to bless you, but your prayers go unanswered? You may think the problem is that God doesn't care. But He does care. . .*very* much. He may just be waiting for you to realize what the problem is, to repent, and clear the blockage out of the channels.

## JEREMIAH 7–8
### Treating Sin Lightly

Jeremiah warned his people to repent of worshipping other gods, but they didn't see it as a big problem. They just made a few small reforms, causing Jeremiah to say that they were treating a deep wound as though it were a mere scratch (Jeremiah 8:11). Are there areas of your life where you need to make major changes—say, what you view on TV or the internet? Or the way you handle your finances? Or the way you talk about family members? Treat serious issues seriously, and God's forgiveness and grace will flow into your life.

## JEREMIAH 9–10
### The Dangers of Gossip

---

A seemingly minor sin had God very upset. The Jews were gossiping about one another—even their close friends and neighbors. They spoke pleasantly to them but were actually seeking dirt and setting traps for them (Jeremiah 9:3–8). Gossiping and badmouthing others is pandemic in today's world also. Some people are nice to your face but cut you down to others. Don't listen to their gossip—and don't copy their habits. It's like catching a terrible disease. The solution is to speak evil of no one and to speak good about everyone (Titus 3:2).

## Not Many Gods

Many ancient peoples worshipped entire pantheons of gods. The Canaanites worshipped about seventy gods, and the Greeks and Romans had myriad deities also. In Jeremiah 11:13 God stated that Judah also had as many gods as it had towns. Today it's common for nominal Christians to say that worship of all these other gods is as valid as worshipping God—that it's "*their* truth." But God says that He won't give His glory to another nor will He share His praise with false gods (Isaiah 42:8). Reserve your praise for Him alone.

## JEREMIAH 13–14
### Wandering from God

In Jeremiah 14:10 the Lord said that His people loved to wander, so He no longer accepted them. There's a big difference between a believer who frequently falls in some area of temptation, is in anguish about it, and prays desperately to change versus someone who has given themselves over to sin. The latter *love* to wander from God. They take delight in sin then brush off conviction from the Holy Spirit, telling themselves that they're fine. As long as you keep your heart tender toward God, He can work in your life.

### Like a Loan Shark

---

No one likes loan sharks or credit card companies that charge exorbitant interest. People don't enjoy watching their hard-earned cash get gobbled by the greedy. Jeremiah warned his people to turn from their evil ways and found himself just as unpopular as a loan shark (Jeremiah 15:10). Have you ever experienced this? You take a stand on a moral issue and the next thing you know, your entire workplace is mocking you. Or former friends exclude you, insult you, and repeat your name with a sneer. Cheer up. You'll be blessed (Luke 6:22–23).

## JEREMIAH 17–18
### Trust in God, Not Man

———◦———

In Jeremiah 17:6–8 the Lord said that the one who trusts in Him will be blessed. He or she will be like a tree planted by the water, whose roots drink in abundant moisture. They won't wither when droughts come. Their leaves will always be green. They will never fail to bear fruit. Does that describe your life? Are you rooted deep in Jesus Christ? Are you cleansed by the Word? (See Colossians 2:7; Ephesians 5:26.) If your roots go down deep in God, you'll still trust Him and experience His joy and blessings when others fade.

........................................................................

........................................................................

........................................................................

........................................................................

........................................................................

........................................................................

........................................................................

........................................................................

........................................................................

........................................................................

# JEREMIAH 19–21
## A Smashed Clay Jar

God told Jeremiah to buy a clay jar from a potter. Then he was to smash it on the ground in front of the elders and priests and give them this message: God will smash Judah and Jerusalem like a shattered potter's jar that can't be fixed (Jeremiah 19:1–2, 10–11). Jeremiah did this to illustrate a message. Do you use visual aids or refer to current news stories to illustrate the truth? Sometimes when people just don't get what you're saying, doing something startling like Jeremiah did helps get the point across.

## Proving You Know God

---

The Lord said that the former king, Josiah, had done what was right and just. He had rendered justice to the poor and the needy. Then God asked if this was not, in fact, what it meant to *know Him* (Jeremiah 22:15–16). Christians who merely promote a social gospel are missing the point, but so are Christians who try to deny the importance of helping their fellow man. You must not merely love them "in your heart" but in practical, material ways as well. Loving your neighbor is a clear way to prove you know God.

........................................................................

........................................................................

........................................................................

........................................................................

........................................................................

........................................................................

........................................................................

........................................................................

........................................................................

........................................................................

## Finding Good in Disasters

When King Jehoiachin, his officials, and the skilled workers of Judah were exiled to Babylon, it seemed like a great disaster—and it was. But God promised that He would watch over these exiles and bring them back, and they would know Him (Jeremiah 24:4–6). What fabulous promises! God works great good even in terrible circumstances. For the same reason, He has promised to chastise you because He loves you, but His discipline produces good results (Hebrews 12:10–11). God always has your best interests in mind.

## God Loves Mercy

---

God is willing to relent from judging people if they change their ways. He told Jeremiah to warn the Jews that disaster was coming then added that if they listened and turned from their evil ways, he wouldn't inflict it on them (Jeremiah 26:2–3). God is more than willing to have mercy on you when you've disobeyed Him. He loves to show mercy, which is why the Bible says that mercy triumphs over judgment (James 2:13). Have you sinned? Although sin grieves your Father, He is ready and willing to pardon you. Turn to Him today.

## JEREMIAH 27–28
### Who Owns the World?

---

In Jeremiah 27:5, God said that He made the earth and all its nations, and that He gives it to anyone He pleases. However, Satan told Jesus the world had been given to *him*, and *he* gave it to anyone he pleased (Luke 4:5–6). God told the truth. Did the devil? Well, the devil may temporarily rule certain people, cities, and nations, but God hasn't surrendered the world to him. God's angels are fighting the devil's fallen angels for control, and though the devil may seem to be winning, God will triumph in the end.

## Praying to Prosper

God sent a message to the Jews living in exile in Babylon. They were to pray for the peace and the prosperity of the city they resided in even though its rulers and people were pagans. God said to pray for it because if *it* prospered, *they* would prosper (Jeremiah 29:7). It's scriptural to pray for prosperity. While God may allow you to endure lack at times, as even the apostle Paul did (Philippians 4:12), overall, it's His will that you can afford your needs and even have more than you need to share with others.

# JEREMIAH 31
## The New Covenant

In Jeremiah 31:31–34, God promised to make a New Covenant with His people. He said He'd write His law on their hearts, forgive their wickedness, and remember their sins no more. This prophecy is quoted in Hebrews 8:8–12, and Hebrews 9:15 says that Jesus established this covenant. You don't need to follow the endless commands and rituals of the Old Covenant (the Law of Moses). You're saved and your sins are forgiven by the blood of Christ. His Spirit dwells in you and makes you alive, so strive to always walk in His Spirit.

# JEREMIAH 32
## Buying a Field

Jerusalem was under siege by enemy armies. Food was running out. Then God told Jeremiah that his cousin was going to offer to sell him a field outside the city, and Jeremiah was to buy it. The field was beyond reach and of no use to Jeremiah now but was a sign that peace and prosperity would return. In your darkest hour when hope seems beyond reach, and you doubt that you'll ever see happy days again, God offers hope. So go ahead—continue to dream. Buy that field. Invest in tomorrow. The future is bright.

## JEREMIAH 33–34
### God's Great Doings

———•◦•———

God encouraged His people to call out to Him, saying that He would answer them and tell them great and unsearchable things they didn't know (Jeremiah 33:3). But you may be weary of petitioning God. Perhaps you've been praying for the salvation of a wayward child for years, and there's no answer yet. Continue to believe that with God, anything is possible. The Lord has also promised to send *you* peace, security, and prosperity (vv. 6, 9). Expect Him to bless you with those even when, at present, you experience anxiety and lack.

## The Only Copy. . .Gone!

Have you ever had a computer crash in the middle of a project and realized it's been *days* since you backed up your work? The prophet Jeremiah once suffered just such a setback. He had sent his only copy of all his prophecies to the king's counsellors, and the king burned the scroll. But God helped Jeremiah remember his prophecies, and God even gave him many new words (Jeremiah 36). Don't despair if you crash—even if you crash and burn. With God on your side, it's not the end. But hey, it's a good idea to back up your work.

## Don't Despair in Darkness

Jerusalem had been besieged for years, and the Jews had used up all the water in Malkijah's cistern. There was only mud in its bottom. One day, Jeremiah's enemies lowered him into that mud and left him to starve in the darkness. But a court official, a Kushite named Ebed-Melek, rescued him. You may feel like you're sinking in mire. You may feel trapped in darkness. It may seem like no one and nothing can help you, but cry out to God. He can rescue you. He can move people's hearts mightily, causing them to act on your behalf.

———•◦•———

As Jerusalem was about to fall, the Jews in the city feared they'd all be slain by the enemy. But God promised Ebed-Melek that though people all around him perished, God would rescue him (Jeremiah 39:15–18). This echoes God's promises in Psalm 91:7–10. Ebed survived because he trusted in the Lord. Many people claim Psalm 91 during times of war or great danger, but it doesn't always work for them. God extends His promises of supernatural protection to those who truly trust Him and who live in obedience to Him, like Ebed did.

## Promises to Obey

———•◦•———

The Jews had a momentous decision to make—either flee to Egypt to escape potential danger or stay in Judah, trusting God to protect them. They asked Jeremiah to pray for them and promised to obey whatever God said. But when He said to stay, they refused to (Jeremiah 42; 43:1–4). How often do God's children promise to obey Him, whether He says yes or no, only to rebel when they don't like His answer? Then they do what they wanted to do all along. You wonder why they bother to ask. Don't be like that.

## Seeing Things Backward

Jeremiah told the Jews that their calamity was punishment for worshipping deities like the Queen of Heaven. But the Jews said that they'd prospered as long as they worshipped her but had suffered lack after being forced to stop (Jeremiah 44:1–3, 15–18). They saw things completely backward. Is there a similar situation in your life? Is a godly friend trying to convince you of something, but you refuse to listen, insisting that the opposite is true? You know, you *could* be wrong. Check it out with your pastor and the Bible.

# JEREMIAH 45–47; JEREMIAH 48:1–13
## Seeking a High Position

———•◦•———

Baruch came from a leading family and might have risen to a high position had he not chosen to become Jeremiah's scribe (Jeremiah 36:4, 17–18). At times though, Baruch still longed for a prestigious career. God told him *not* to seek such things because He was about to destroy Judah. You may not have to turn down a life of wealth, fame, and power, but as a Christian determined to follow Christ, you can identify with Baruch. You too must continually choose God's will over the fleeting things of this world (see 2 Peter 3:11).

## Moab's Pride

---

How do you feel when an arrogant person is wealthy and secure and mocks your faith? Maybe you wonder why the ungodly are "blessed" while you struggle financially. The Jews wondered that about the Moabites, who were mocking Judah's troubles from their high plateaus. God assured the Jews that He was aware of Moab's haughtiness (Jeremiah 48:29–30). But like bullies today, her insolence was futile and her boasts accomplished nothing. Trust in God. When the bullies are plucked from their lofty heights and brought down to the dust, you'll still be standing.

## Settling Accounts

God had ordained that Babylon invade Judah as punishment for her sins even though the Babylonians were proud, cruel pagans. But Babylon acted in excessive wrath so much so that she opposed God's purposes. So He saw to it that she was judged too (Jeremiah 50:24–26). You might have an overseer at work who is making your life miserable not because of any sin on your part but because God is allowing you to be tested. Stay faithful. God will eventually deliver you and settle accounts with those who oppress you.

# JEREMIAH 51:1–44
## Raising Up Rescuers

Jeremiah contains precise prophecies. In Jeremiah 51:11 and 28, the prophet declared that the Lord would use the Medes to destroy Babylon. Sure enough, seventy years later the Medes joined the Persians, and Darius the Mede conquered Babylon and became its ruler (Daniel 9:1). When you're in the midst of confusion and frustration, and a fellow believer encourages you to cheer up because God will deliver you, you might think that it sure doesn't look like it. But God already knows exactly how He will do it even if you have no idea who He plans on using.

## Honor Despite Humiliation

In Jeremiah 24:4–6, God said that King Jehoiachin (who had gone into exile) was like good fruit. The prophet Ezekiel viewed the deposed Jehoiachin as Israel's true king (Ezekiel 1:2). And God saw to it that the king of Babylon eventually bestowed honor on Jehoiachin (Jeremiah 52:31–34). Like Israel's exiled king, you may have been fired or laid off your job (whether unfairly or not) and may be in humble circumstances now. But God is able to care for you and restore your honor even if He doesn't restore you to your former situation.

........................................................................................

........................................................................................

........................................................................................

........................................................................................

........................................................................................

........................................................................................

........................................................................................

........................................................................................

........................................................................................

........................................................................................

# LAMENTATIONS

Although the prophet Jeremiah had warned the southern Jewish nation, Judah, to obey God, they didn't repent, and now the prophet witnesses the punishment he'd threatened. God allows the aggressive, expanding Babylonian Empire to conquer Judah because of her sins. Many of her people are taken as captives to faraway Babylon (Lamentations 1:5). The sight of his nation crushed brings tears to Jeremiah's eyes (1:16), hence his nickname, "the weeping prophet." Lamentations ends with a cry to God, who Jeremiah feels is furious with His people and has rejected them.

## LAMENTATIONS 1–2
### Interceding in the Night

Have you ever woken up extra early and been unable to fall back asleep, despite your best efforts? To make matters worse, a troubling situation or a certain person keeps cycling through your thoughts. If so, God wants you to pray. In Lamentations 2:19, God told His people to arise and cry out to Him in the night, to pour out their hearts like water in His presence. So rise up! Take the opportunity to intercede. You might even be moved to tears. God knows, you can always catch up on your sleep later.

## LAMENTATIONS 3–5
### God Doesn't Afflict Willingly

After Jerusalem fell to the Babylonians, many Jews were killed. The few survivors were in desperate straits. Judging by the anger and violence of their conquerors, it seemed as if God had abandoned His people. After all, He had *told* them He was angry with them. But Lamentations 3:31–33 assures you the Lord doesn't cast off believers forever. Though He allows you to suffer grief, because of His great unfailing love, He will show compassion on you. Know this: God doesn't willingly bring affliction or grief on you.

# EZEKIEL

Ezekiel is exiled to Babylon at the same time as King Jehoiachin and becomes God's spokesman to his fellow exiles. He shares unusual (even bizarre) visions with the people, reminding them of the sin that led to their captivity and telling them that He will bring further judgment on the Jews in Judah. But he also offers hope of restoration. Because the Jews are refusing to listen to verbal warnings, God leads Ezekiel to perform a number of silent skits to drive the message home. A vision of a rebuilt temple dominates the last chapters of Ezekiel.

## EZEKIEL 1–2; EZEKIEL 3:1–14
### The Cherubim

---

In the book of Ezekiel—and in Revelation—fantastic monsters called cherubim are described surrounding the throne of God. They have heads of lions, men, eagles, and oxen; six wings; and eyes covering their bodies. These creatures serve as the honor guard and praise choir of the Almighty, never ceasing to praise God day or night. The Lord has created some absolutely astonishing creatures that nearly defy description and baffle the mind. The good news is the same marvelous, creative God is at work in your life today, doing miracles that you can barely dream of.

..................................................................................

..................................................................................

..................................................................................

..................................................................................

..................................................................................

..................................................................................

..................................................................................

..................................................................................

..................................................................................

## Ezekiel's Silent Skits

———— ·•· ————

God frequently sent prophets to warn His people, but they didn't always listen. So God had Ezekiel do a series of silent skits to get their attention (Ezekiel 4:1–17; 5:1–12). Only *after* doing pantomimes did the prophet explain their meaning. You may be frustrated that God answers your prayers for direction with mysterious signs, leaving you to decipher their meaning. You may wonder, "Why can't God just speak *English*?" But God even spoke to Bible prophets in various ways (Hebrews 1:1). Why? Sometimes when you're forced to really think about things, you get the meaning even clearer.

## EZEKIEL 6–7
### Worthless Gold and Silver

———— ·◦· ————

Ezekiel said the day would come when the Jews would toss their silver and gold into the streets. They had made idols out of that gold and silver, and in their day of desperate need, those idols couldn't save them. So they hurled them away in anger (Ezekiel 7:19–21). You may place a high value on material things—particularly money—only to find out in a crisis that they can't solve life's most pressing problems and can't buy off your troubles. So call out to God when problems assail you. He's your only sure source of help.

## EZEKIEL 8-10
### Idolatry in the Temple

———•◦•———

God carried Ezekiel away in the spirit to the temple at Jerusalem, where He showed the prophet four different instances of His people worshipping idols (Ezekiel 8:1–16) right in the temple of God! So the glory of God departed from the temple (8:6; 10:18–19). It takes a lot to anger God to the point that His judgment is inevitable. It takes a lot of unrepentant sin for the presence of God to depart from His people. God has shown you great mercy, so respond to His lovingkindness and wholeheartedly seek His face today.

# EZEKIEL 11–12
## True and False Prophets

Ezekiel declared that God would judge the Jews still in Judea and exile them to Babylon also (Ezekiel 12:10–20). But false prophets were saying the opposite: that God would bless and keep the Jews in Judea and soon even let the exiles in Babylon go home (Jeremiah 28:1–4). Like Ezekiel's day, there are false prophets in the churches, blessing the greedy and the selfish. Many people who don't want to put up with sound doctrine anymore listen to teachers who say what their itching ears *want* to hear (2 Timothy 4:3). Who do you listen to?

...........................................................................................................................

...........................................................................................................................

...........................................................................................................................

...........................................................................................................................

...........................................................................................................................

...........................................................................................................................

...........................................................................................................................

...........................................................................................................................

...........................................................................................................................

...........................................................................................................................

## EZEKIEL 13–14
### Whitewashing Weak Walls

Judah's false prophets were saying that everything was fine with their nation's moral fiber, but Ezekiel said they were like unscrupulous workmen who instead of fixing a weak, tottering wall, painted it with whitewash to make it look strong and new (Ezekiel 13:10–16). Are there situations in your home, your workplace, or your church that desperately need attention? Are you ignoring a problem because it would just take too much time and effort to fix it or there's too much resistance to change? What wall might you be whitewashing?

## Useless Burned Junk

---

God asked Ezekiel if wood from a grapevine was ever used to make something useful. The answer was no, not even pegs to hang things on. It was too weak. Well then, what about after it was burned in the fire? No. It would be even weaker and *less* useful then (Ezekiel 15:1–5). Now, think of this useless wood as being like so many of the habits, pastimes, and values of your old life. So many of your former, sinful ways are of no value in your new life with Christ. Leave them laying back in the ash heap.

## Old Testament Parables

Jesus was a master teacher and storyteller and engaged His audiences with vivid, fascinating but mysterious parables. But He wasn't the only one to use parables to drive His points home. In these chapters, Ezekiel speaks of eagles and trees and branches and harlots. God also teaches you today with a story whose meaning is often hidden. What story is that? The story of your own life. Sometimes even Jesus' more cryptic parables are easier to understand than what God is doing in your heart. But keep on learning. The story's not over yet.

## EZEKIEL 18–19
### Sins of the Fathers

———

In chapter 18, the prophet challenged one of the Israelites' pet doctrines—generational curses. The Jews back then misunderstood Exodus 20:5 to mean that children inevitably suffered for the sins of their ancestors. No matter how righteous they were, the curses of the past bound them. But God corrected them, saying that people are either blessed or cursed because of their *own* deeds. It doesn't matter how sinful your parents were. If you sincerely love Christ and obey Him, He has broken the curses of your past when He Himself took on your sins and became a curse for you (Galatians 3:13).

........................................................................

........................................................................

........................................................................

........................................................................

........................................................................

........................................................................

........................................................................

........................................................................

........................................................................

# EZEKIEL 20
## Sweet-Smelling Saints

The Israelites had sinned repeatedly against the Lord. Nevertheless, God promised that when He gathered them from distant nations and brought them back to their own land, He would cleanse them of their sins and accept them as an offering of fragrant incense (Ezekiel 20:41). Though you too have sinned, know this: when you accepted Christ as Savior, God removed the filthy garments from you, clothed you in pure robes of righteousness, and made you to smell like the pleasing aroma of Christ (2 Corinthians 2:15). Stay close to Jesus so His scent lingers on you.

## God Gives Guidance

God had determined that Jerusalem would be judged. When the king of Babylon stopped at a fork in the road to seek an omen—whether to attack Jerusalem or Rabbah—he cast lots with arrows. God made sure that he chose the arrow marked "Jerusalem" (Ezekiel 21:21–22). Today superstitious people still make life and death decisions based on the flip of a coin or by drawing straws. God *may* wink at such ignorance (Acts 17:30) and give you an answer that way, but He'd much rather you received guidance from His Word and His Spirit.

## The Angry Furnace

God said that just as impure silver is thrust into a fiery furnace to melt it and separate the precious metal from the dross, so He judged His people in the heat of His anger (Ezekiel 22:17–22). But His end purpose was loving—His painful chastisement purified them and made them better. God judges sin, and though His hand is heavy upon you and the fiery trial you're going through seems to only show that He's angry and is rejecting you, in the end you'll be better for it (Hebrews 12:11).

---

Ezekiel's wife was "the delight of his eyes." Every time he looked at her, he was delighted. One morning the Lord told him that she would die, and that same evening it happened. God told Ezekiel not to weep, so he didn't (Ezekiel 24:15–18). Sometimes the cost of following God can be steep. Jesus said that His disciples must love Him more than they loved their wives (Matthew 19:29). To be clear, the Bible commands men to love their wives as much as they love themselves (Ephesians 5:28). But they are to love God more.

In Ezekiel 26:4–5, 12–14, God said men would pull down Tyre's walls, towers, and houses and throw her stones into the sea, leaving only bare rock where men would spread fishnets. Armies would then plunder her wealth. Nebuchadnezzar demolished Tyre in 572 BC, but the Tyrians fled with their wealth to an offshore fortress island. But in 332 BC, Alexander's Greek army cast the rubble into the sea, making a causeway out to the island, which they then looted. For centuries, fishermen spread their nets to dry on the causeway. You serve a mighty, all-knowing God.

# EZEKIEL 28–29
## Pride and Downfall

Tyre and Sidon were merchant cities on the coast north of Israel. Their ships sailed all over the ancient world, so the people were immensely wealthy, wearing costly apparel and gems. As a result, they were filled with pride. Ezekiel 28:1–19 describes the doom of Tyre's king, and verses 12–17 are widely believed to also be another description of the devil's fall from heaven. Like the king of Tyre, he was judged when he became proud of his great beauty and splendor. Christians are warned by this example to not get lifted up in pride (1 Timothy 3:6).

## EZEKIEL 30–31
### Egypt's Glory Fails

———————

In a vivid parable, God described Assyria as a towering, luxuriant cedar tree, the envy of all the trees of Eden (once-exalted nations). But despite all its glory, Assyria was cut down and fell into darkness, joining them in the realm of the dead. When you die, no worldly beauty, achievements, or glory will matter anymore. Jesus asked what profit would it be to you if you have it all in this life and are held in great honor and esteem, yet lose your own soul? (Mark 8:36). Make sure to live your life for God.

## Watchman on the Wall

---

Ezekiel 33 describes God's call to the prophet Ezekiel to be a watchman on the city wall, eyes wide open and alert, on the lookout for approaching enemies. He was responsible to warn the people of coming danger. If you're a parent, you too are a watchman, a lookout, for your children. It is your responsibility to warn them of the dangers that others can bring into their lives as well as the consequences of their own actions. Your children may not always heed your warnings, but it's your job to warn them anyway.

## Pretty Love Songs

The Israelites came and sat before Ezekiel, listened to his warnings, and said they loved God, but they refused to change their greedy, dishonest lifestyles. They heard his words but didn't obey them, so Ezekiel was nothing more to them than a talented musician singing pretty love songs (Ezekiel 33:30–32). Guard against complacency, lest you find yourself going to church every Sunday, enjoying the music, but not truly surrendering your life to God or taking the pastor's message to heart. Jesus' teachings aren't always easy to obey, but determine to obey them.

These chapters contain two verses of deeply moving, beautiful promises. In Ezekiel 36:26–27, God promised that He would give you, His child, a new, soft heart. He also promised that He would put His Holy Spirit in you and move you to follow His commands and make you desire to carefully keep His laws. It's wonderful knowing that you don't have to "work up" the will to obey God. He will stir up your spirit by His Spirit and *make* you want to obey. So pray that He moves in you.

# Valley of Dry Bones

This is one of Ezekiel's most bizarre visions, but it's filled with tender, beautiful meaning. In Ezekiel 37, God said that these bones were the people of Israel. They were complaining that their bones were dried up, meaning that their hope of being restored to God's good graces was gone. They felt He was irrevocably angry with them. So God showed them this wasn't so. You may feel condemned about your past sins, convinced that God will always be angry at you. Cheer up! Have hope! God has forgiven you. He hasn't forsaken you.

## Invasion of Israel

---

Ezekiel 38 and 39 describe an invasion of Israel by a great northern power. Ezekiel 38:2 speaks of a "chief prince" (prince of Rosh), and many Christians believe this refers to Russia. But chapter 39 speaks of heaps of wooden weapons burning, so it doesn't sound like modern warfare. These chapters make for interesting speculation, but too often people have entrenched doctrinal interpretations for them and quickly get into arguments. God's servants, however, are not to quarrel (2 Timothy 2:23–24). Instead, you are to love people and gently use scripture to persuade them.

## The New Temple

Beginning with chapter 41, the next several chapters describe a temple of God. Since this temple doesn't match the temple Zerubbabel built—which Herod later enlarged—it may well describe the temple the Jews will soon build to replace the one the Romans destroyed. We don't really know. The detailed descriptions of the height and width of every wall, pillar, and object read like architectural guidelines, but the exact purpose of certain things in the Bible isn't always clear. God has a purpose for them, however, so leave this mystery in His hands for now.

## EZEKIEL 42–43
### God's Glory Returns

Earlier, Ezekiel had described the glory of God about to leave the temple in Jerusalem (Ezekiel 8:1–6). Now Ezekiel 43:1–7 describes God returning to the temple and His glory filling it. Then he heard God declaring that this was again the place of His throne where He would dwell. Have you endured the termination of a dream or a ministry for God due to human error or sin and been overcome with joy when it revived? Just because it seems like the end of a dream doesn't mean it's dead forever. God can revive it.

## Serving God Close Up

---•◦•---

With God's presence returned to the temple, God restored the Levites who served in His inner courts. In the past, many Levites had compromised with idolatry, so their descendants could only serve at the altar outside the temple or as guards at the doors. But those who truly loved and obeyed God could serve in the holy places (Ezekiel 44:10–16). An ancient psalmist declared that he yearned to be in God's presence. Do you long to be close to God? Or are you content to be a doorkeeper? Even that is blessed (Psalm 84:2, 10).

## Cooking Offerings

Did you ever wonder where all the meat was cooked and broiled when dozens of people were offering at the temple at once? Surely not on the *one* altar of burnt sacrifices! In Ezekiel 46:21–24, the prophet describes many kitchens attached to the temple's outer court. Just when you think the Bible is describing something that wouldn't work, God provides an explanation. Are there mysteries or confusing points in the Bible that you worry might be contradictions? Don't worry. They're perfectly rational when He shines a little more light on them.

# EZEKIEL 47–48
## The River of Life

Ezekiel had a vision of a river flowing out of God's temple from south of the altar. The river grew in volume and depth as it flowed toward the Dead Sea, and trees grew in profusion on its banks. This water made the stagnant sea come alive with fish (Ezekiel 47:1–9). John later described the River of Life flowing out of the throne of God, with Trees of Life growing along its banks. This appears to be the same river, and God invites you to drink deeply of its waters and live (Revelation 22:1–2, 17).

# DANIEL

Daniel, along with three other Jewish youths, is taken from Judea to serve the king of Babylon. Daniel's ability to interpret dreams endears him to the king. Shadrach, Meshach, and Abednego refuse to bow before a golden idol and are thrown into a blazing furnace where the Lord keeps them safe (Daniel 3:25). A later king, Belshazzar, sees handwriting on the wall, which Daniel interprets as their imminent conquest by the Medes. The Median king, Cyrus, makes Daniel an advisor but is tricked into sending him to a den of lions. God protects Daniel even there.

## DANIEL 1; DANIEL 2:1–30
### Taking a Stand

———•◦•———

When Daniel and three friends went into training for the king's court, Nebuchadnezzar assigned them food from his own table. But to obey Jewish dietary laws, the four youths resolved not to defile themselves by eating the royal food (Daniel 1:5, 8). Likewise, the early Christians were advised not to eat food dedicated to pagan gods (1 Corinthians 8:1–13; 10:25–33). If you have dietary scruples or have stated you won't watch certain movies, be sure to follow through. Otherwise people will think you're insincere or may become emboldened to cross the line themselves.

## DANIEL 2:31–49; DANIEL 3
### Refusing to Bow Down

King Nebuchadnezzar had a golden idol made and commanded his subjects to worship it or be thrown into a fiery furnace. Daniel's three friends refused, saying that God could protect them but that even if He chose *not* to, they still wouldn't bow down to the king's idol (Daniel 3:17–18). Are you willing to take a bold stand—to refuse to bow down to the idols of this present age, trusting that God will protect you, but that if He doesn't, you're willing to suffer the consequences? What issues are you prepared to stand for?

# DANIEL 4
## The Insane King

One day Daniel warned the king that if he didn't change his ways, God would humble him. Sure enough, after Nebuchadnezzar boasted about building the magnificent city of Babylon, God caused his mind to snap, and for years the king lived and ate like a wild animal. God is able to humble you too if you become proud of your looks, your talents, or your accomplishments. So give God the glory. Let people know that you're nothing without Him and that He's the one using you to do great things (John 15:4–5).

## Writing on the Wall

When Belshazzar was king, Babylon was besieged by the Medes, but he threw a great party. In the middle of the celebrations, God sent a disembodied hand to write a mysterious warning on his wall. The writing warned Belshazzar that he was about to lose the kingdom. What "handwriting on the wall" are *you* presently seeing but failing to understand? Are you oblivious to the state your finances are in? Are you ignoring signs of rebellion in your children? Are you drifting away from God in some area? It doesn't pay to ignore warning signs.

## DANIEL 6:18–28; DANIEL 7
### Knowing the Future

The prophet Daniel had amazing dreams about four awe-inspiring, fearsome creatures. God was telling him what the future held. People want to know what's going to happen. That's why they go to fortune-tellers, have their palms read, or scour Nostradamus's quatrains for obscure messages. Many Christians develop an excessive interest in Daniel and Revelation and live their whole lives expecting the imminent rise of the Antichrist. It's fine to be interested in the future, but learn to strike a balance. Make sure you also follow Christ's simple teachings and live for Him *today*.

## Prayer of Repentance

---

In Daniel 9:4–19, Daniel took ownership of the Israelites' sins and rebellion against the Lord then came before God representing His people and interceded for them. Daniel stated that he and his people didn't make requests because they were righteous but because of God's great mercy (v. 18). God answered Daniel's prayer, and He can answer yours too if you sincerely intercede for your nation. God has a set time in which He has determined to send blessings upon His people. If they haven't come yet, will you pray for God to send them?

........................................................................................................

........................................................................................................

........................................................................................................

........................................................................................................

........................................................................................................

........................................................................................................

........................................................................................................

........................................................................................................

........................................................................................................

........................................................................................................

........................................................................................................

## Spiritual Warfare

---

Daniel fasted and prayed for three weeks. Then the angel Gabriel appeared and told him that from the first day he began praying, God had heard him. But the demon prince of Persia had resisted Gabriel for twenty-one days (Daniel 10:12–13). Demons are still battling angels in the heavenly realms, which is one reason it sometimes takes *your* prayers quite a while to be answered. God hears you and may send the answer immediately, but sometimes you need to fight in prayer and stand your ground, expecting, if you are to see the answer established.

## The Resurrection

The angel told Daniel that multitudes who were dead would one day rise—the righteous to eternal life, the unsaved to judgment. In that day, the wise and those who win souls for God's kingdom will shine like stars (Daniel 12:2–3). Are you living for Jesus, yielding to Him in every area of your life, being an example to unbelievers, and sharing how they too can experience a new life in Christ? If so, be encouraged! God will greatly reward you one day soon. You'll be glad for all eternity that you lived for Jesus.

# HOSEA

God gives the prophet Hosea a strange command; he is to marry a woman known to be promiscuous (Hosea 1:2). Their marriage is to be a picture of God's relationship to Israel—an honorable, loving husband paired with an unfaithful wife. Hosea marries an adulteress named Gomer and starts a family with her. He's never quite sure if the children she bears are his. When Gomer returns to her life of sin, Hosea—again picturing God's faithfulness—buys her back from the slave market. Much of the book contains God's warnings regarding disobedience but also His promises of blessing for repentance.

## HOSEA 1–3
### God's Faithfulness

God told Hosea to marry a promiscuous woman and have children with her because, like an adulterous wife, the land of Israel was unfaithful to the Lord. Even after she left him for another man, the Lord told Hosea to receive her back and love her as He loved the Israelites (Hosea 3:1). God forbid that your mate should stray—even in their imagination—but would you be willing to forgive them? In fact, can you forgive them for the times they ignore you, seem disinterested, and are caught up in some other pursuit?

## HOSEA 4–7
### Love Like Morning Mists

Hosea said that when his people sought the Lord, they couldn't find Him. Why? He had withdrawn from them because they weren't sincerely seeking Him but worshipped other gods in their hearts. Their professed love for God didn't last long. It was like a morning mist, like dew that disappeared as the sun rose (Hosea 5:4, 6; 6:4). How about you? Is your love deep and sincere? Does it hold steady through life's long day? If so, you'll encounter God when you seek Him. If you don't at first, persist. Seek wholeheartedly and you'll find Him (Jeremiah 29:13).

## HOSEA 8–10
### Plow Your Heart

————•◦•————

After a long summer of drought, the ground in Israel became hard and difficult to plow. But when the winter rains had fallen, the earth was soft. So God advised people to seek Him and ask Him to send rain so they could plow, plant, and reap a harvest (Hosea 10:11–12). God longs to send showers of His righteousness upon your life but often withholds them for a time to cause you to turn to Him in prayer. Then, after His refreshing rains come, new life springs up and you reap the fruit of His unfailing love.

..................................................................................................................

..................................................................................................................

..................................................................................................................

..................................................................................................................

..................................................................................................................

..................................................................................................................

..................................................................................................................

..................................................................................................................

..................................................................................................................

..................................................................................................................

## HOSEA 11–14
### Your Loving Father

In Hosea 11:3–4, the Lord said that it was He who taught Ephraim (northern Israel) to walk, taking him by the arms. God was like someone who lifts a little child to their cheek, who bends down to feed him. The apostle Paul set a similar example, saying that he had dealt with new Christians as a father with his children, encouraging, comforting, and urging them to live lives worthy of God (1 Thessalonians 2:7, 11–12). May you know the tender love of God your Father, and may you be an example of His love to others.

# JOEL

❧❧❧

A devastating locust swarm descends upon the nation of Judah, but the prophet Joel indicates this natural disaster is nothing compared to the coming great and very terrible day of the Lord (Joel 2:11). God plans to judge His people for sin, but they still have time to repent, and obedience will bring both physical and spiritual renewal. God promises that He will pour out His Spirit on all mankind (2:28). When the Holy Spirit comes on Christ's disciples at the Feast of Pentecost (Acts 2), the apostle Peter quotes this passage from Joel to explain what has happened.

## A Gracious, Loving God

Israel had sinned grievously against the Lord, but He promised that even now if they returned to Him with all their heart, He would refrain from sending judgment. After all, He was gracious, compassionate, slow to anger, and overflowing with love (Joel 2:13). How would you describe the nature of God in *your* life? Have you found Him to be gracious and full of tender mercies? Have you experienced His abundant love and deep compassion? Spend time with Him in prayer today and ask Him to reveal His heart to you.

## God Restores Fortunes

———

After waves of locusts had ravaged their land, setting them back years, Joel told the Israelites to rejoice in the Lord. Why? Because God had promised to send such abundant rain and harvests that they'd recover from the years the locusts had eaten (Joel 2:21–26). Have you suffered misfortune? Have you experienced a lack of God's blessing? Turn to Him, surrender to His will, and then pray for Him to reimburse you for *your* years the locusts have eaten. Then wait and see what the Lord will do. And rejoice in Him.

# AMOS

An average guy named Amos—a lowly shepherd and orchard keeper—takes on the rich and powerful of Israelite society, condemning their idol worship, persecution of God's prophets, and cheating of the poor. Though God once rescued the people of Israel from slavery in Egypt, He is ready to send them into new bondage because of their sin. Amos sees visions that picture Israel's plight: a plumb line, indicating the people are not measuring up to God's standards, and a basket of ripe fruit, showing the nation is ripe for God's judgment.

## AMOS 1-4
### A Special Relationship

---

In Amos 3:2, God told the Israelites that He had chosen only them out of all the nations of the earth, and He'd therefore punish them for *all* their sins. This was because they were in a covenant relationship with Him, sworn to obey Him. As a Christian, you have a new covenant relationship with God through Jesus Christ. His Spirit has entered your heart, making you God's son or daughter. This relationship also allows Him to be intimately involved in how you live your life. That's why He lets you get away with a lot less than the unsaved.

## AMOS 5–7
### When the Lord Relents

Twice the Lord showed Amos that He was about to send judgment on Israel—first a locust swarm, then a vast fire—and twice the prophet pled for Him to forgive. Both times, God relented and said this judgment wouldn't happen (Amos 7:1–6). You may think, like Amos, that you're utterly insignificant, a nobody. Why would God bother listening to you? But every believer, even the weakest Christian, has the potential to influence the actions of God, whether He sends judgment on people, situations, and nations or has mercy. So pray!

## AMOS 8–9
### Famine for God's Word

———•◦•———

As a dry land with slight rainfall, Israel often experienced drought and famine. But the Lord warned that He was about to send a different kind of famine—a famine of His Word. People would wander everywhere, searching for a new revelation from God, but wouldn't find it (Amos 8:11). God has sent you the living Word, His Son, Jesus Christ, to give you eternal life and to reveal God to you. Stop wandering to and fro, checking out cheap imitations. Draw near to God in His secret place, and find peace with God through Jesus Christ.

(*Read this entry together with the entry from Obadiah.*)

........................................................................................................

........................................................................................................

........................................................................................................

........................................................................................................

........................................................................................................

........................................................................................................

........................................................................................................

........................................................................................................

........................................................................................................

........................................................................................................

# OBADIAH

❧——❧

Edom is a nation descended from Esau—the twin brother of Jacob, the patriarch of Israel. The baby boys struggle even in their mother's womb (Genesis 25:21–26), and their conflict continues during their lives and between their descendants over the centuries. After Edom takes part in the Babylonian ransacking of Jerusalem, Obadiah passes down God's judgment: for their violence against their kinfolk, the Edomites will be overwhelmed with shame, and God will cause them to cease from being a nation (Obadiah 10). It sometimes takes a while for God's judgments to catch up to the wicked.

# OBADIAH
## Not Too High for God

————◦•◦————

Edom was a land of high plateaus and nearly inaccessible cities like Petra, and the Edomites boasted that no foreign army could conquer them. But God told them that though they soared like an eagle and made their nest among the stars, even from there He'd bring them down. No matter how impregnable you think you are, you're not beyond God's reach. So beware of becoming proud, for He's able to humble you. Better to humble yourself and to dwell in the high and holy place with God, the High and Lofty One (Isaiah 57:15).

.................................................................................................................

.................................................................................................................

.................................................................................................................

.................................................................................................................

.................................................................................................................

.................................................................................................................

.................................................................................................................

.................................................................................................................

.................................................................................................................

.................................................................................................................

# JONAH

God tells the prophet Jonah to preach repentance in Nineveh, capital of the Assyrian Empire. Jonah disobeys, sailing in the opposite direction to Tarshish (southern Spain). A storm rocks his ship, and the desperate sailors finally throw him into the sea. He then spends three days in a giant fish's belly before deciding to obey God. The creature vomits Jonah onto a beach, and he starts walking to Nineveh. When Jonah preaches, all Nineveh repents, and God spares the city. But the prejudiced prophet pouts. The story ends with God proclaiming His concern even for pagans.

# JONAH 1–4
## Jonah's Complaint

Jonah had a complaint against the Lord. He said he'd known *all along* that God was a gracious, compassionate God, slow to anger, and abounding in love, a God who relented from sending calamity (Jonah 4:2). *That's* a complaint? Yes, and it really bothered Jonah. Sometimes you too may be disappointed with God when He fails to strike down the wicked, especially if those wicked have trampled on you or yours. You may wish for God to exact justice. Have both love and faith. One day, God will judge them. But today may not be that day.

# MICAH

Micah is a Jew from the small town of Moresheth in southern Judah. He lives at the same time as the great prophet Isaiah and sees firsthand how the poor are suffering under the hands of wealthy oppressors. He therefore chastises both the northern and southern Jewish nations for pursuing false gods and cheating the poor. Micah warns that the two nations will be devastated by invaders (the Assyrians) and predicts the fall of Samaria (the northern capital), but he promises that God will preserve the remnant of Israel (Micah 2:12).

# MICAH 1–4
## Doctrines They Love

The people of Israel were selfish, self-consumed, and corrupt. They weren't interested in the Word of God. Micah sized them up right when he said that if someone prophesied that they'd have plenty of wine and beer, that he'd be just *their* kind of prophet (Micah 2:11). Do you have similar inclinations? Do you seek comfort, security, and "the good life" above all? Are you eager for prosperity doctrines that allow you to set your heart on worldly riches to the detriment of deeper spiritual growth and a strong witness for the Lord?

## MICAH 5–7
### God's Simple Requirements

———•◦•———

The Law of Moses had a multitude of rules but at its heart was very simple. This is why Micah could say that God had shown His people what was good and that He only required them to act justly, to love mercy, and to walk humbly with God (Micah 6:8). Jesus said that all the Law was summed up in these two commands: love God with all your heart, and love your neighbor as you love yourself (Matthew 22:37–40). It's great to get into in-depth Bible studies, but never forget the simplicity of God's Word.

# NAHUM

About 780 BC, the prophet Jonah warns that God is about to destroy Nineveh, capital of the cruel Assyrian Empire. When Nineveh repents, God has mercy on them. But the Assyrians return to their brutal ways, so about 640 BC, God sends the prophet Nahum. This time Nineveh's doom cannot be averted. "Woe to the bloody city!" Nahum cries (Nahum 3:1). Nineveh is targeted for judgment by God, who will demolish them in the sight of all nations being oppressed by her. Nahum's prophecy comes true when the Babylonian Empire overruns Nineveh in 612 BC.

## NAHUM 1–3
### Mighty Nineveh Falls

Nineveh was the unconquerable capital of the Assyrian Empire, but Nahum prophesied that the river gates would be thrown open and the city would fall (Nahum 2:6). In 612 BC, enemy armies released a dammed-up river, washing away the defensive wall, and the city was taken. God often prophesied that the impossible would happen. A mighty empire would fall. A proud city would be sacked. These things seemed highly unlikely at the time, but the prophecies were all fulfilled. You can trust that God will bring justice, hope, and peace to today's troubled planet as well.

# HABAKKUK

In Judah, a prophet named Habakkuk complains that God is allowing violence and injustice among His people. But Habakkuk is then shocked to learn the Lord's plan for dealing with the problem: to send the violent Babylonians to punish Judah (Habakkuk 1:6). Habakkuk argues that the Babylonians are even worse than the disobedient Jews and basically says, "You wouldn't really be able to stand having them work for You, would You?" (1:13). The Lord, however, says He's only using the Babylonians for His purposes and will in time punish them for their own sins.

# HABAKKUK 1-3
## Happy in Desperate Times

In Habakkuk 3:17, the prophet states that even though his fig trees don't bud, there are no grapes on his vines, his olive crop fails, the fields produce no food, and all his sheep and cattle die, he will still be joyful in the Lord. You may wonder if such a statement reflects reality. Could you *really* be happy if the world fell into deep depression and you had nearly nothing? You may reason no, but think again. You can be happy even during times of need, knowing that you have an everlasting inheritance in heaven.

# ZEPHANIAH

Zephaniah, a man of Judah evidently related to the royal family, begins his book with a jarring prophecy that states in the second verse that God is about to consume every living thing from the land. People, animals, birds, and fish will all perish, victims of God's wrath over Judah's idolatry. Other nearby nations will be punished as well in the fire of God's wrath (Zephaniah 3:8). But there is hope: in His mercy, God will one day restore a remnant of Israel that will neither practice iniquity nor speak lies (3:13).

## ZEPHANIAH 1–3
### God Sings for Joy

Zephaniah 3:17 states that the Lord God is with you. He will take great delight in you, and in His great love for you, He will no longer judge you. Instead, He will rejoice over you with singing. Does this describe *your* relationship with God? Do you believe that God takes great delight in you? Do you believe His heart is filled with great love for you? Can you actually picture Him rejoicing over you—literally singing for joy? If you don't see God that way, ask Him to open your eyes to it.

# HAGGAI

One of three postexilic prophets, Haggai encourages Jews who were once Babylonian captives to restore the demolished temple in Jerusalem. The new world power, Persia, has allowed the Jewish people to return to Jerusalem; but they are distracted with building their own comfortable homes, saying that the time to build the Lord's temple hasn't come yet. Through Haggai, God tells them that the reason they are suffering a drought that is parching the countryside and diminishing their wealth is because they need to rebuild the temple first. Then God will once again send rain and bless them.

## HAGGAI 1–2
### Doing God's Work

The Jews were back in their land, but times were tough. They expected much but ended up with little. What they brought home, God blew away. Why? Because the Israelites were all busy with their own houses. Meanwhile, God's house, the temple, was still in ruins (Haggai 1:2–6). It's fine to work hard at your job, to earn a good wage, to have a nice home, and own fine things, but don't focus on your own life to the exclusion of God's work. Don't neglect the needs of the church or other needy Christians.

# ZECHARIAH

❧ ⸱⸱⸱ ❧

Like Haggai, another postexilic prophet, Zechariah, urges the Jewish people to rebuild the temple. He also has amazing visions of different-colored horses and of a golden lampstand and two olive trees. He gives several prophecies of the coming Messiah, including an end-time vision of a final battle over Jerusalem when the Lord shall go forth and fight against the nations. Zechariah declares that the Lord's feet shall stand upon the Mount of Olives, which will then split in two, creating a great valley. Then the Lord shall be king over all the earth (Zechariah 14:3–4, 9).

## ZECHARIAH 1–3
### When Foes Go Too Far

———•◦•———

In Jeremiah, God described how Judah's idolatry had so angered Him that He had sent the Babylonians to conquer them. But in Zechariah 1:14–15, God said He was even angrier with Babylon. He had only been a little angry with His people, but the Babylonians had gone *too far* with the punishment. God didn't intend them to commit war crimes. It's good to remember that when watching the news, God isn't behind the atrocities. He punishes sin, yes, but He's loving. Knowing this ought to resolve some issues you have with God.

## ZECHARIAH 4–7
### God Will Do It

Zerubbabel had led the Jews in starting to rebuild the temple, but then enemies forced them to stop. Now God told them it was time to finish building it. He told Zechariah that this work would not depend on human might or power but on His Spirit (Zechariah 4:6). This is a key thought for you too when facing your day's work and problems. You can't just depend on your own strength and ability. You won't win by forcing the situation. You will succeed only if God is working in you and through you.

## ZECHARIAH 8–9
### God Comes to Bless

———————

You read in Jeremiah and 2 Kings how God was determined to bring disaster on His people and how He showed no pity after they had angered Him. But now, after they had returned to their land, God was determined once again to do good to them. Always remember that His anger lasts only a moment. Then it comes to an end and passes. Meanwhile, His favor and love for you lasts your entire lifetime. You may be weeping for a night when God is chastising you, but you'll be rejoicing again by morning (Psalm 30:5).

## Rain in Its Season

In Israel, the former rains come in late autumn/winter, and the latter rains come in spring. Zechariah 10:1 tells you to ask the Lord for rain in the springtime because that's a season He has ordained for it to come in. It still arrives on schedule. If the rain runs a little late, well, *pray* for God to send it. But you shouldn't expect days of heavy showers in the middle of summer's drought. There are seasons to life too. That's why you can't always hurry God when you're praying for Him to do a miracle.

## ZECHARIAH 13–14
### End-Time Earthquake

———◦•◦———

Zechariah 14:4 says that in the last day, the Lord will stand on the Mount of Olives, east of Jerusalem, and it will be split in two, forming a great valley. Like so many events in Bible prophecy, we can't be certain when this will happen, though it likely occurs when Jesus returns to fight the Battle of Armageddon in a great valley (Revelation 14:17–20; 16:16; 19:14–15). Keep an open mind regarding the interpretation of these verses. You'll know when you *need* to know. In the meantime, love God and your fellow man.

# MALACHI

Prophesying a century after the return from exile, Malachi chastises the Jews for offering crippled and sick sacrifices to the Lord (Malachi 1:8); for divorcing their Jewish wives to marry pagan women; and for failing to pay tithes for the support of the priests and the temple. The Lord is angry with the attitude "It's vain to serve God" (3:14), but He promises to bless the obedient, saying to those who fear His name that the Sun of righteousness shall arise with healing in His wings (4:2). Malachi also gives a prophecy about John the Baptist (4:5–6).

## MALACHI 1–4
### Always Excusing Yourself

In this book, God repeatedly lays charges at the feet of His disobedient children only to have them constantly ask, "How have we done that?" (See Malachi 1:7; 2:13–14, 17; 3:7, 8, 13.) They acted so innocent, protesting that they weren't doing anything wrong. It would have been funny if it hadn't been so sad. Do you sometimes have that attitude? When a friend or family member—or even God—points out an area where you're falling short, do you constantly justify yourself and ask, "Who, me?" It's better to take His admonition to heart and change.

# MATTHEW

The first of the four Gospels, Matthew is written to a Jewish audience and quotes numerous Old Testament passages to prove that Jesus is the promised Messiah. Beginning with a genealogy that shows Jesus' ancestry, Matthew details His miraculous conception and the visit of the wise men. Jesus' teachings and parables are emphasized, including His Sermon on the Mount (chapters 5–7) and the Lord's Prayer. As with all four Gospels, Matthew details the death, burial, and resurrection of Jesus; he is the only biographer of Jesus to mention several miracles that occur at that time (Matthew 27:50–54).

## Born of a Virgin

———•❖•———

God prophesied that a virgin would give birth to a child named "God with us" (Matthew 1:22–23). But did you know that Jesus *had* to be born of Mary's family line (Luke 3:23–38) and not Joseph's (Matthew 1:1–16)? Joseph was descended from David through Jeconiah, and none of Jeconiah's descendants would sit on David's throne (Jeremiah 22:24–30). So Jesus *had* to be conceived in Mary's womb by the Holy Spirit. It should thrill you to know that God watched over these details. He watches over many details in your life as well.

## Sermon on the Mount

Jesus' teachings in Matthew 5–7 are called the Sermon on the Mount, and this wasn't the only time Jesus taught these things. He likely repeated these basic truths often in different cities, villages, and open-air settings. Jesus taught that you are to live your entire life motivated by love. You are even to love your enemies. You are to trust God for your needs and selflessly help others when asked to. You are to obey these teachings of Jesus wholeheartedly. Many of these truths are quite difficult to live, but they're important.

## MATTHEW 6–7
### The Lord's Prayer

Jesus taught a simple, all-encompassing prayer in Matthew 6:9–13. On another occasion, He taught a slightly different version (Luke 11:2–4). That shows that He didn't mean for you to simply memorize it and quote it unthinkingly, but to use it as a guideline in communicating with your Father. This prayer reminds you to praise God, to yield to His will, to resist temptation, to trust God for your daily needs, and to forgive others. If you constantly meditate on these things, you'll be filled with the Lord's love and Spirit.

## The Faith of the Centurion

A Roman centurion once asked Jesus to heal his servant but knew that Jews couldn't enter Gentiles' homes (Acts 10:28). So he said for Jesus to simply speak the word from a distance, and his servant would be healed. Jesus praised the centurion's great faith (Matthew 8:5–13). Sometimes you may think that you have very small faith, since you don't normally trust God to do great miracles, but just the same, steadily commit your cares and needs to Him day after day. And read His Word faithfully, because it's the Word that increases your faith (Romans 10:17).

# Sending Out the Twelve

One day Jesus appointed twelve disciples to be apostles ("sent-out ones"), to heal the sick, cast out demons, and preach the Gospel (Matthew 10:1–6). God has also given *you* talents, skills, and spiritual gifts and sent you into the world to represent His kingdom, to tell people about Him, to help others, and to make the world a better place. You may not think you have much to offer, but if you're doing what God wants you to do, He will do what you can't do, and bring about the desired effects.

# MATTHEW 12
## Mercy and Grace

———•◦•———

While Jesus and His disciples were passing through a field, they plucked some grain, rubbed off the husks, and ate it (Matthew 12:1–8). The Pharisees said that this simple act was "work," so they accused them of breaking God's law that said not to work on the Sabbath. But Jesus said that God desired mercy more than rigorous adherence to rules (v. 7). Jesus, in fact, ushered in a whole new approach to life. For though the Law was given through Moses, grace and truth came through Jesus Christ (John 1:17). So walk in His grace.

# MATTHEW 13
## The Parable of the Sower

---

Have you ever pondered what kind of soil most resembles *your* life? Are you like the hard-packed path—someone who doesn't understand the truth so never takes it deep into your heart? Are you like stony soil with little depth—someone whose lack of commitment doesn't allow the Word to get deep roots? Are you like the soil full of thorns, whose preoccupation with wealth or worldly cares chokes out the seed? Or are you like the good soil that causes a great, rich harvest to come up (Matthew 13:1–9, 18–23)?

.............................................................................

.............................................................................

.............................................................................

.............................................................................

.............................................................................

.............................................................................

.............................................................................

.............................................................................

.............................................................................

.............................................................................

## Moved by Compassion

Once Jesus miraculously fed five thousand people. He had taken His disciples to a desolate region to rest, but the people followed Him there, so Jesus was moved with compassion on them and healed their sick. He also had compassion on them and fed them (Matthew 14:13–21; Mark 8:2). Like Jesus, there may be times when you wish to rest, to get away to recuperate. But needy people place demands on you. What do you do? By all means rest if you can, but also be ready to take action if God moves you with compassion.

## A Steadfast Understanding

In Matthew 16:13–20, when Peter stated that Jesus was the Messiah, the Son of God, Jesus said God had revealed this to Peter. Thus, many people think this was the first time Jesus' disciples realized who He was. But they *already* knew this fact three years earlier (see John 1:49). It's one thing to have a revelation of who Jesus is, in all His power and glory, in your early fervor as a believer. It's very desirable to still have this understanding of His identity and power after many of life's setbacks. Is your faith still burning brightly?

...................................................................................................

...................................................................................................

...................................................................................................

...................................................................................................

...................................................................................................

...................................................................................................

...................................................................................................

...................................................................................................

...................................................................................................

...................................................................................................

# MATTHEW 18–19
## *Importance of Forgiveness*

In the parable of the unmerciful servant (Matthew 18:21–35), Jesus taught on the importance of forgiving others. He said that God would punish people if, after being forgiven by Him, they stubbornly refused not only to *forgive* their brother or sister but to forgive *from the heart*. Whatever form you believe this punishment will take, one thing is clear: loving and forgiving others is an integral part of the teachings of Him whom you call Lord and Master. Jesus knows it's not always easy to forgive others, but He requires it just the same.

## MATTHEW 20; MATTHEW 21:1–27
### A Mother's Request

———•◦•———

We don't know if James and John decided that they deserved exalted thrones then asked their mother to speak for them or whether it was her idea and they went along with it. Either way, Salome was an ambitious woman who spoke her mind (Matthew 20:20–28; Mark 10:35–37). If you grew up with a dominant, outspoken parent, you can identify with this. Your parent greatly desired for you to succeed, pushed you to rise, and sometimes tried to live their dreams through you. Pray about which of these attitudes to retain and which to set aside.

......................................................................................

......................................................................................

......................................................................................

......................................................................................

......................................................................................

......................................................................................

......................................................................................

......................................................................................

......................................................................................

......................................................................................

## The Wedding Banquet

———— •◦• ————

The most poignant verse of this parable in Matthew 22:1–14 describes how, after being invited to the royal wedding, the king's subjects paid no attention but instead went off to their regular work, one to his field, another to his business (v. 5). They had no time for their king. Does this sometimes describe your days? Are you too busy with work, family, friends, and other responsibilities and interests that crowd out time with the King? Make time for the Lord today. Give Him the priority He deserves. You won't regret it.

## An Angry Jesus

Matthew 23 is Jesus at His sharpest. He rails against religious hypocrites, calling them a brood of vipers and asking how they expect to escape the fires of hell. This is a little-explored aspect of the Lord's divine personality. Yes, the same Jesus who tenderly blessed children and forgave those who crucified Him will one day thunder down to Armageddon in righteousness, judging hypocrites and making war on evil people. You can be thankful Jesus hates wickedness. You'd have long ago been overwhelmed by the evil one if Jesus wasn't so passionate about it.

## Sheep and Goats

Matthew 25:31–46 is an unvarnished parable with a strong message about loving your fellow man, even the most despised. It also contains beautiful promises, so that the total effect is that of a lovely rose crowning a barbed stem. Jesus doesn't mince His words regarding the love and self-sacrificial action He expects from His disciples. At times, you might even wish that He had toned things down a bit, not been quite so stern. But He's the holy Son of God. You are to bow down and worship Him, not question Him or put Him on mute.

## The Plot against Jesus

The chief priests hated Jesus and plotted to kill Him but realized they needed to do it secretly. Jesus was greatly loved by the common people for the same reason the rulers hated Him: He was an outspoken critic of hypocrisy. The working class listened to Him *gladly* (Mark 12:37). Do you gladly listen to Jesus, or at times do you find some of His zingers striking uncomfortably close to home? Jesus calls you to be zealous like He is and repent of insincerity and double standards. Keep things simple. Love and follow Jesus' teachings.

When Jesus was crucified like a common criminal, He seemed to be a weak, ordinary man not the eternal, triumphant Son of God. His Father appeared to have deserted Him, and as He hung dying on the cross, Jesus groaned, "My God, my God, why have You forsaken me?" (Matthew 27:46) Second Corinthians 13:4 assures you that though Jesus was weak when He was crucified, He now lives eternally by the power of God. Though you also are weak, you too shall live with Him by the same power. Walk in His Spirit today.

# MARK

The Gospel of Mark is the briefest of the four biographies of Jesus. Mark addresses a Gentile audience, portraying Jesus as a man of action, divinely empowered to heal the sick, control nature, and battle the powers of Satan. Mark's theme of the suffering servant comes through in Jesus' interaction with hostile doubters—the Jewish leaders, who want to kill Him (Mark 9:31); His neighbors, who take offense at Him (6:3); and even His own family members (3:21). The abasement of Jesus pictures this truth: whoever desires to be great should become the servant of all (10:43–45).

## MARK 1–2
### Called to Follow

———•◦•———

The first you hear of Peter and Andrew in Mark's Gospel is when Jesus commands them to follow Him, and they immediately leave their jobs and follow Him (Mark 1:16–20). He wasn't a stranger to them, however. They'd known Him for a full year already and already knew He was the Messiah (John 1:35–42). Jesus usually works that way in your life. He doesn't give you a cold call. He lays the groundwork to prepare you for ministry or to go on mission trips, etc. You've had time to get to know Him. Now will you follow Him?

## Jesus Calms the Storm

———•◦•———

Jesus and His disciples were crossing the Sea of Galilee when a furious storm rose, and the waves broke over the boat, nearly sinking it. Jesus ordered the storm to stop, and it did. Then He asked His disciples where *their* faith was. They could have done it too. You may wish you had Jesus physically present to deal with all your problems. Well, when He went away, He sent His Spirit into your heart (John 16:7). This means that Jesus' miracle-working power is available to you also. You just need to pray in faith.

..............................................................................................

..............................................................................................

..............................................................................................

..............................................................................................

..............................................................................................

..............................................................................................

..............................................................................................

..............................................................................................

..............................................................................................

..............................................................................................

## Power over Evil Spirits

When Jesus sailed to the far shore of the Sea of Galilee, He was met by a man possessed by a legion of demons. Now a legion was five thousand soldiers, which is why this man had the strength to snap iron chains. Yet He was terrified of Jesus (Mark 5:1–20). Don't get so focused on the power of the devil that you forget that Jesus is *much more* powerful. The Bible assures you that you can overcome the evil one because greater is Christ in you than all the evil spirits in the world (1 John 4:4).

## Rash Vows

---

Herod had imprisoned John the Baptist for denouncing his immoral marriage to Herodias but protected John when his wife wanted to kill him. But one day Herod made a rash oath and was forced to behead John (Mark 6:14–29). Have you ever painted yourself into a corner by speaking without thinking about your words? Proverbs 6:1–5 urges you to take steps to free yourself from such promises if at all possible. It's better, of course, to refrain from making rash statements in the first place (Ecclesiastes 5:5–6).

...........................................................................................

...........................................................................................

...........................................................................................

...........................................................................................

...........................................................................................

...........................................................................................

...........................................................................................

...........................................................................................

...........................................................................................

...........................................................................................

...........................................................................................

## Praying within God's Will

At first glance, it appears that this Greek mother outwitted Jesus by talking Him into granting her request with her quick answer. But what happened was that Jesus rewarded the humility of a woman willing to identify herself with dogs. And He honored her tremendous faith (Mark 7:24–30). You may feel that you must overcome God's reluctance when you pray and talk Him into giving you something He doesn't wish you to possess. This is the wrong attitude. You must pray in faith for things that are, after all, within His will for you to have.

# MARK 9
## The Transfiguration

Jesus was atop a mountain with three disciples when His robes began blazing with light and His face shone like the sun (Mark 9:2–8; Matthew 17:2). God *told* them that Jesus was His Son (v. 7), and He wished to *show* them as well. You probably won't see Jesus in His glory in this life like they did (2 Peter 1:16–18), but God tells you also that Jesus is His Son and that you're to listen to Him. You listen to Him every time you read His words in the Bible and seek to obey them.

# MARK 10
## Wealth and the Kingdom

It almost sounds as if Jesus was telling the rich young ruler that in order to be saved, he had to sell all his possessions and give the money away (Mark 10:17–31). No. Jesus was saying that if the man did that, he'd have *rewards* in heaven (v. 21). His salvation was a separate issue. Note that Jesus said it was impossible for *anyone* to be saved (vv. 26–27), rich or poor. Only *God* can save you. True, if you have riches, it's harder to trust God, but the poor have trust issues as well.

## Judgment of the Fig Tree

Jesus once walked up to a fig tree to look for fruit but found none, so he cursed it. Its leaves *immediately* withered. By the next morning, the entire tree had withered from the *roots on up* (Matthew 21:18–20; Mark 11:12–23). Jesus cursed the fig tree as a symbol of doomed Israel. For three years, Jesus had come looking for fruit on it, but found none, so the time for judgment had come (Luke 13:6–9). Sure enough, disobedient Israel was destroyed by the Romans within forty years. Be zealous to obey God and bear the fruit of His Spirit.

# The Greatest Commandments

When asked which of God's commands was the greatest, Jesus named *two* commands not one. The first one was to love God wholeheartedly; the second was to love your neighbor as you love yourself (Mark 12:28–34). Why did Jesus quote *two* commands? Because many people claim to love God but actually don't love or know Him. But if you fulfill the *second* command, it provides clear, tangible proof that you have fulfilled the *first* command (see 1 John 3:16–18; 4:7–8, 11–12). The importance of the second command, therefore, can hardly be overstated.

## MARK 14
### Prayer in Gethsemane

When Jesus entered the Garden of Gethsemane (Mark 14:32–42), He told His disciples Peter, James, and John to watch and pray so that they wouldn't fall into temptation. Their spirits were willing to stand strong, but their flesh was weary and weak (v. 38). You too must pray so that God can help you stand firm and so you won't waver in times of temptation or testing (Ephesians 6:12–13). God is able to strengthen you with might by His Spirit in the inner person (3:16). Pray for His strength today.

*Jesus Before Pilate*

------•◦•------

Pilate heard how many things Jesus' enemies were accusing Him of and marveled that He didn't debate their charges. But Jesus said nothing (Mark 15:3–5). This fulfilled Isaiah's prophecy that like a sheep is silent before its shearers, so the Messiah would not open His mouth (Isaiah 53:7). Many Christians, however, rush to speak in their own defense. Many times it's wise to give thought to what you'll answer those who ask questions (1 Peter 3:15). However, at times you're not to premeditate what you'll say, but trust God to give you the words (Matthew 10:19–20).

# LUKE

***

Luke's Gospel is addressed to a man named Theophilus (Luke 1:3) to create an orderly declaration of those things believed among Jesus Christ's followers (1:1). Luke's book is the least Jewish and most universal of the four Gospels. Luke shows Jesus' compassion for all people: Roman soldiers (7:1–10), widows (7:11–17), the "sinful" (7:36–50), the chronically ill (8:43–48), lepers (17:11–19), and many others—including a criminal dying on a cross (23:40–43). As with all the Gospels, Luke shows Jesus' resurrection but adds His appearance to two believers on the Emmaus road.

# LUKE 1
## Just Like Your Dad

———•◦•———

Has anyone ever pointed out that you make the same facial expressions or the same sounds as your dad? You may have inherited his corny sense of humor, attitude, or habits. Zechariah was a righteous man, but he had a tendency to rationalize and question even after receiving a divine revelation (Luke 1:6, 18–20). His son, John, also had a divine revelation, and he too doubted (John 1:29–34; Luke 7:16–19). Be thankful if you inherit *good* tendencies. An inquiring mind can be good too, so long as you know when to question and when to trust.

.................................................................................................

.................................................................................................

.................................................................................................

.................................................................................................

.................................................................................................

.................................................................................................

.................................................................................................

.................................................................................................

.................................................................................................

.................................................................................................

## LUKE 2
### Forced to Choose

———◆◆◆———

Simeon told Mary that her child would cause either the rise or the fall of people, and because of Him, the thoughts of many hearts would be revealed (Luke 2:34–35). If you choose Jesus, you'll be blessed by God and will one day rise in glory. If you reject Him, you'll stumble over Him and fall (Romans 9:33). When confronted with Jesus' claims, you're forced to choose, and on judgment day, the secrets of your heart will be revealed. It's wise to have chosen Jesus, but it's important to *continue* to choose His ways in every decision, large and small.

## Supernatural Signs

God had told John that He'd recognize the Son of God when he saw the Spirit descend and remain on Him (John 1:32–33). Sure enough, after John had baptized Jesus, he saw heaven open and the Holy Spirit flutter down on Jesus in bodily form like a dove (Luke 3:21–22). It's wonderful when God grants you a supernatural sign to give you wisdom and guidance, but you can't always count on those. Usually God requires you to figure things out or seek wisdom in others' counsel. Be thankful if He gives you signs as well.

## Jesus, Friend of Sinners

Jesus ministered largely in Galilee, and this disgusted His opponents, who considered Galileans to be second-class Jews. But what *really* offended them was when they saw Jesus eating and drinking with tax collectors and prostitutes. But Jesus had come to heal the spiritually sick (Luke 5:27–32). Are you involved in prison ministries? Do *you* have a heart for social outcasts, the marginalized and the overlooked of your city? Do you have compassion on the mentally handicapped? You can't spend time with everyone, but you *can* show love and kindness to everyone you meet.

## LUKE 6; LUKE 7:1–18
### Love Your Enemies

———————

Jesus shocked people when He told them to love their enemies, to do good to those who hated them (Luke 6:27–28). This command continues to surprise people. Worse yet, Jesus repeats it a few verses later and tells you how to love your enemies—to lend to them knowing that you probably won't get your belongings back (v. 35). How can you have *that* kind of illogical love? By living near to the heart of your Father. He shows kindness to the wicked and the unthankful, and as His child, you should too.

..................................................................................................

..................................................................................................

..................................................................................................

..................................................................................................

..................................................................................................

..................................................................................................

..................................................................................................

..................................................................................................

..................................................................................................

..................................................................................................

## Anointed by a Harlot

Jesus had been preaching to a crowd and made a point of saying that God loved and forgave even despised sinners (Luke 7:34). A harlot of that city believed Him. So when Jesus went into a house to eat, she followed Him and wept over His feet, washing them with her tears (vv. 36–50). Jesus praised her faith—childlike, she believed God had forgiven her sins—and her great love (v. 47). Do you believe that Jesus has forgiven your sins—*all* of them? Does your faith move you to do deeds of love?

## A Light Touch

———•◦•———

As Jesus was walking along, the crowd nearly crushed Him. No wonder Peter was surprised when Jesus asked, "Who *touched* me?" (Luke 8:41–48). Many people had. But a sick woman had merely brushed her fingertips against the edge of His robe—in faith—and Jesus had felt healing power leave Him. You can manhandle Jesus in demanding prayer all day, and nothing will change; but if you believe—if you have real faith—the *merest touch* will bring a surge of His power into your life and answer your whispered prayer.

........................................................................

........................................................................

........................................................................

........................................................................

........................................................................

........................................................................

........................................................................

........................................................................

........................................................................

........................................................................

........................................................................

## Be a Good Samaritan

Did the Levite and the priest fail to help the wounded Jew because they didn't care? It's possible they *did* care, and their consciences bothered them. But because the man was half-dead, they didn't want to become ceremonially unclean and be unable to serve in the temple for seven days if he died in their hands (Numbers 19:11). Don't let legalistic rules hold you back from reaching out to the needy in love. Don't become so focused on "serving God" or being involved in Christian activities that you don't reach out to an unsaved neighbor. Be a Good Samaritan (Luke 10:29–37).

## LUKE 11
### Persist in Prayer

In Luke 11:5–10, Jesus said that if you need bread to feed a guest at midnight, knock and keep on knocking on your neighbor's door. Even if he tells you no at first, he'll eventually get out of bed to give you what you need. Jesus didn't mean that your Father is a tired, grumpy neighbor; He was stressing the importance of persistence in prayer. For everyone who asks—and keeps on asking—receives. In Isaiah 62:7, the prophet tells God's people to give Him *no rest* until He mightily blesses Jerusalem.

# LUKE 12
## Don't Worry

---

Jesus teaches you not to worry about what you will eat or wear. He assures you that if you seek God's kingdom first, He will see to it that you lack nothing (Luke 12:22–34; see also Matthew 6:25–34). You may feel this is impractical—that life simply wouldn't work if you give no thought to daily matters. But Jesus wasn't saying not to plan or to give thought to your responsibilities. He meant not to give anxious, troubled thought to them. You are to prepare, do your best, then trust God to bless you.

## The Gospel Yeast

In Luke 13:21, Jesus said the kingdom of God was like yeast that a woman mixed into about sixty pounds of flour. (She must have been the town baker.) She pummeled and massaged it until she had thoroughly worked the yeast into the dough. In the same way, you are to accept God's Word and His Spirit and allow them to permeate every corner of your life so that they guide your every decision. You are to beware of the yeast of hypocrisy (Luke 12:1) but gladly accept the yeast of the Gospel.

## Costs to Be a Disciple

⸻•⸻

As Jesus was going from town to town, large crowds traveled with Him. He was the greatest show in Israel, told fascinating stories, and performed miracles. They were happily following Him now but planned to soon return to their homes, families, and occupations. Then, as now, Jesus reminds those who would follow Him that being His disciple means putting Him before your loved ones, careers, and material possessions. It means surrendering your entire life to Him. It involves self-sacrifice (Luke 14:25–33). Are *you* a dedicated disciple, yielding every aspect of your life to Christ?

....................................................................................

....................................................................................

....................................................................................

....................................................................................

....................................................................................

....................................................................................

....................................................................................

....................................................................................

....................................................................................

## The Kingdom Within

One day the Pharisees asked Jesus when the kingdom of God would come, and He replied that (for the present, that is) its coming wouldn't be a major, observable event, nor could they point to any town and say, "There it is!" But the kingdom of God must begin in individual, transformed lives (Luke 17:20–21). Like the Jews, you may be waiting for God's physical kingdom to come upon the earth—and it *will* tangibly arrive one day—but for now, focus on becoming a loyal citizen of God's invisible kingdom.

## Seeking Restitution

---

For minor, everyday offenses, Jesus commands you to frankly forgive. Believers are not to go through life holding on to petty, personal offenses. But what do you do if the offense is major and life-altering and the offender never apologizes, never makes amends? Jesus told a parable about a widow insisting that a judge render her justice, and while this parable is chiefly about persistent prayer, its point is that you are to persist in praying for *justice*. You have legal rights under the law and do well to avail yourself of them (Luke 18:1–8; Acts 16:35–39).

## The Triumphal Entry

When Jesus rode a donkey down the Mount of Olives and into Jerusalem, multitudes of Jews proclaimed Him the Messiah. And when He seized control of the temple courts, they expected His kingdom to be set up then and there (Luke 19:29–46). But Jesus had to die for humanity's sins first. Even today, the Son of God often confounds expectations. You expect a sudden healing, a miraculous deliverance, or global peace, but your situations continue unchanged. . . for now. God's way of working out problems is far above your way (Isaiah 55:8–9).

## The Last Supper

During this last Passover meal, Jesus handed His disciples bread, saying this was His body broken for them, and He gave them wine, saying that this was His blood poured out for them (Luke 22:14–20). He'd explained earlier that these things gave them eternal life (John 6:53–56). Communion is a holy event, rich with meaning, and whenever you celebrate it, you declare that you are one body with Christ and one with all your fellow believers (1 Corinthians 10:17). This is a time to forgive offenses, to apologize to those you've hurt, and to pray for unity.

## LUKE 22:39–23:33
### Laying Down Your Life

Jesus and His disciples went to the dark hillside garden, where Jesus prayed. He knew He'd suffer for many hours and wished to avoid it, but He also knew that this was the only way He could pay for your sins. So, moved by love, He yielded to His Father's will (Luke 22:39–44). John wrote that this is how you know what love is—by the way Jesus laid down His life for you. Therefore, you also ought to lay down your life for others, even when it causes you discomfort or pain (1 John 3:16).

## He Walks with You

———•◦•———

When He walked the road to Emmaus with two disciples, this wasn't the first time that Jesus had traveled incognito (John 7:8–10). By taking on a disguise, He was able to lay a foundation of teaching in their hearts (Luke 24:13–27). You may wish that the Lord would walk with you through the lonely, painful paths of life. He does. In Genesis 28:15, He assured Jacob that He was with him and would watch over him wherever he went. And in Hebrews 13:5, He promised that He would never leave nor forsake you.

# JOHN

·······

While the books of Matthew, Mark, and Luke have
many similarities, the book of John is unique. The
fourth Gospel features none of Jesus' parables and
few of His miracles. Instead, John provides extensive
treatments of Jesus' reasons for coming to earth and
speaks often of His deity. Jesus came so that we might
have life and have it more abundantly (John 10:10). He
had an intimate relationship with the Father, saying
that He and His Father were one (10:30). John also
shows Jesus' patience with Thomas, who doubted
the resurrection (20:24–29), and Peter, who denied
the Lord (21:15–23).

## JOHN 1–2
### The Word Become Flesh

This Gospel declares up front that Jesus Christ is far more than a man but is united in deity with His Father (John 1:1–14). It states that Jesus (here called the Word) was with God in the beginning and *is* God. We know from Genesis 1:1 that God created the heavens and the earth, and John states that God created all things through Jesus. This means that you are to worship Jesus as God. And think of it! When you have the Spirit of Christ in your heart (Galatians 4:6), you have the infinite, eternal God Himself dwelling inside you.

*Simple Salvation*

---

John 3:16 is one of the simplest, most beautiful verses in the Bible. It states that God deeply loved everyone in the world and proved it by giving His one and only Son, so that whoever believes in Him won't perish but will have eternal life. When you're going through times of deep discouragement and the devil nearly has you convinced that God couldn't love *you* and hasn't saved *you*, quote this verse. And quote Acts 2:21, which says that *everyone* who calls on the name of the Lord will be saved. That includes you!

## Saved Not Judged

Jesus said that if you hear Him and believe in God who sent Him, you have eternal life—already *have* it! You won't be judged but have *already* crossed over from death to life (John 5:24). One day you'll appear before Jesus and be rewarded. Only the unsaved will be judged and condemned (vv. 28–29). Knowing that your name is already written in the Book of Life ought to free you from frustration, anxiety, and ulcers. You don't need to *help* Christ save you by being super-good and obedient either. Just rest in Jesus and trust Him!

This beautiful word picture is found in one of Jesus' most shocking sermons. In it, Jesus said that He was the bread from heaven and that, unless you ate His flesh, you'd never have eternal life. That's what you're doing symbolically when you partake of communion. Many people mentally assent to Jesus. That's like chewing the bread of life. But it won't do you any good unless you swallow it and allow it to nourish your body. You must not only believe in the Son of God intellectually but must receive His Spirit into your very heart.

## Who Is Jesus?

———•◦•———

In Jesus' day merciful, commonsense people, judging by His teachings and miracles, said that Jesus was a good man. Legalistic, unmerciful people, judging Him for healing on the Sabbath and being seen with tax collectors and sinners, argued that He was, in actuality, a deceiver (John 7:12). People's opinions of Jesus reveal a lot about themselves. This is true for you today. If you see Jesus as angry and swift to punish, it will affect your entire outlook and life. If you see Him as merciful and loving, it will affect you in a positive way.

## Continually Pleasing God

Jesus said that God the Father who had sent Him was also *with* Him. God hadn't left Jesus to make it through life on His own. Why? Because Jesus always did what pleased His Father. He always obeyed Him (John 8:29). Of course, God is loving and has mercy on you and forgives you when you repent after straying, but you gain great peace and power if you consistently do what pleases Him. In Acts 5:32, Peter said that God gives the Holy Spirit to those who obey Him. The more you obey, the more of His Spirit you have.

## JOHN 10; JOHN 11:1–27
### The Good Shepherd

———•◦•———

In John 10:1–16, Jesus called Himself the Good Shepherd whose voice the sheep recognize, who leads them out to pasture, and who gives His life to protect them. God's Word has many such allegories. In Psalm 23, David stated that the Lord was his shepherd. (See also Psalm 95:7.) In Luke 15:4–6, Jesus describes a sacrificial shepherd searching for a lost sheep. Do you picture the Lord this way? Do you envision Him as a tender, caring, sacrificial shepherd who loves you enough to die for you? He truly loves you that much.

## The Extravagant Gift

Jesus came to Bethany and was eating dinner when one of his hostesses, Mary, took a pint of costly perfume, poured it on His feet, and proceeded to wipe them with her hair. It was a very extravagant act, and Jesus, who knew He'd soon die, commended her (John 12:1–8). Do you give to the Lord generously and extravagantly? Do you have special talents that you can use to show God your love? Do you care for the poor, the needy, the handicapped, and others whom Jesus loves? You can show Him your love in many different ways.

## JOHN 13–14
### When God Reveals Himself

———————

Have you ever prayed for God to show Himself to you, to reveal His holiness and glory to you? Moses did (Exodus 33:18–23). King David did and caught a glimpse of God's beauty (Psalm 27:4). God longs to let *you* see Him too. Jesus said that the pure in heart will see God (Matthew 5:8). And Jesus said in John 14:21 that if you keep His commands, it's proof that you love Him. And if you stir up your love for Him, He will be moved with love for you and reveal Himself to you.

## Grapevine and Branches

In John 15:1–8, Jesus explained that He was the grapevine, and His disciples were the branches. His Father cuts off every branch that bears no fruit and prunes every branch that does bear fruit to make it even more fruitful. Pruning can be a painful process. You may be nurturing useless activities on the side, and if they're taking up your time and energy but bearing no fruit for God's kingdom, they're likely to feel His blade. You may find yourself arguing against His attempts to clean the clutter out, but let Him have His way.

## Peter's Denial

Peter's denial of Christ appears in all four Gospels. Why do all of them describe his failure? Possibly because God wanted everyone to know that the great things Peter did later—miracles and leadership—were accomplished by God's grace and power not by any strength Peter had. There may be great blots on *your* record of serving God, and you may wonder why He didn't keep you from failing so you'd have a better testimony. Know this: God uses broken, imperfect men and women who can identify with the imperfect sinners they're called to reach.

## The Death of Jesus

Jesus was in terrible pain, barely able to focus or speak during his final hours. He wasn't engaged in normal conversation or lighthearted banter. Each word He said cost Him dearly. So as you read what He spoke, you get a clear idea of what was vitally important to Him. Some of His final words were "It is finished" (John 19:30). The Greek words He spoke were commonly used in reference to a debt that had been paid in full. That was the moment He finished paying the price for your sin and brought about your salvation.

## JOHN 20:11–31; JOHN 21
### Jesus Appears to Mary

———•◦•———

Many Christians believe that Mary Magdalene was once a prostitute. She may have been, but the Bible doesn't ever say that or even hint at it. It says that she was a wealthy woman who had somehow allowed demons into her life but that Jesus then delivered her (Luke 8:1–3). It's worth noting that Mary was the first person to see and touch Jesus after He rose from the dead (John 20:11–18). Your past, no matter how sordid it was, is forgiven in Christ. You are now free to draw near to a holy, loving God.

# ACTS

❧⚬❧

Officially called "Acts of the Apostles," this book is a bridge between the story of Jesus in the Gospels and the life of the church in the epistles. Luke begins with Jesus' ascension into heaven (Acts 1:3). God sends the Holy Spirit on the day of Pentecost, and the church is born. The disciples are empowered to preach boldly about Jesus, and Jewish leaders begin persecuting believers. One persecutor, Saul, becomes a Christian after meeting Jesus on the road to Damascus. Saul, later called Paul, then joins Peter and other Christians in preaching, working miracles, and strengthening the fledgling church.

## ACTS 1–2
### Power of the Spirit

---

After the Holy Spirit fell on the disciples, they miraculously spoke in the languages of visitors from far-flung lands. Peter then preached boldly to these crowds. Jesus had promised that His disciples would receive power when the Spirit came on them, and that happened (Acts 1:8). You receive a *measure* of the Spirit at salvation (Ephesians 1:13; 4:30), but Paul encourages you to be *filled* with the Spirit (Ephesians 5:18). Ask the Lord to daily fill you full to overflowing with His Spirit of wisdom and power. You need Him to live an effective Christian life.

## ACTS 3–4
### Choosing to Obey God

---

After the disciples told others about Christ, the religious leaders ordered them to stop. Peter and John answered that God had commanded them to preach, and they had to obey Him. Besides, they were full of their subject and couldn't stop speaking about it (Acts 4:18–19). You may not be a dominant personality who enjoys public speaking, but God has promised to fill your heart with His love by His Spirit. This love will then motivate you to be a witness for Christ both by your words and your personal example (2 Timothy 1:7).

## ACTS 5-6
### Persecuted for Christ

Jesus had promised His disciples that if religious foes persecuted Him, they would persecute them as well—and this now happened to them. After being beaten, the disciples rejoiced that they'd been counted worthy of suffering disgrace for Jesus (John 15:18–20; Acts 5:40–41). Are you suffering persecution or insults for His sake? At times it's very painful or embarrassing. It can cost you friends and relationships, but you have to stand up for what you believe in. If you do, the Lord will reward you greatly (Luke 6:22–23).

## ACTS 7
### When Dreams Die

Moses knew God had promised to deliver the Hebrews from slavery and was convinced that God would use *him* to do it. But Moses went about it the wrong way, his own people rejected him, and his dream died and stayed dead for forty years (Acts 7:6–7, 17, 23–30). Were you once convinced that God wanted to use *you* to accomplish something special? Have your dreams died? God is able to resurrect them—and if they were *His* inspiration and not just your own idea, He may yet do it.

## Witnessing to the Nations

Some translations say the eunuch Philip met was from Ethiopia; others say he was from Kush (modern Sudan). Both African nations were converted to Christianity early on. And God didn't send Philip to these lands; He brought the eunuch to Judea (Acts 8:26–39). These days, God is doing something similar: He has brought unevangelized people from many distant nations to your country, your city, and even your neighborhood. You need not leave your homeland to fulfill the Great Commission—preaching the Gospel to all the world (Matthew 28:19; Mark 16:15). Are you seizing this opportunity?

## Peter's Paradigm Shift

———— ◆ ————

Peter was a faithful Jew, so he had never eaten nonkosher food and had never visited an "unclean" Gentile (Acts 10:14, 28). He thought going into all the world to preach the Gospel (Mark 16:15) meant going to the Jewish communities scattered abroad. God had to take Peter through a paradigm shift. How might your own traditions and limiting doctrines be holding you back from reaching out to those who need the Gospel or a demonstration of Christian love? Ask God to lead you daily and constantly show you new things. He's very willing.

## Surprised by Answered Prayer

Peter was arrested and kept in prison, so the church prayed desperately for him. After an angel freed him, he ran to the house where his friends were praying. When a servant insisted Peter was at the door, they said she was out of her mind. They couldn't believe it was him (Acts 12:1–17). How many of your own prayers are like that? Have you ever prayed and prayed for something, then when someone told you your prayer had been answered, you were skeptical? You are to *believe* that you'll receive what you're praying for (Mark 11:24).

## To Blind a Sorcerer

When the sorcerer, Elymas, blasphemed the Gospel, Paul looked straight at him and told him he'd go blind—and instantly he did (Acts 13:4–12). You may wish you had that kind of power to confound your enemies and defend the Gospel from its critics. You *can* have a greater anointing of God's Spirit on your life, but there's a high price tag: You must love and be deeply committed to the Lord, obedient to Him in all things, and be persistent in prayer. And you must believe. All this requires great self-sacrifice.

## Salvation by Grace Alone

One day, Jewish believers came to Antioch from Jerusalem. They taught the Gentile Christians that unless they became circumcised and kept the Law of Moses, they couldn't be saved. Paul strongly argued that faith in Jesus and God's grace was what saved Gentiles *and* Jews. In modern times, people add different manmade commandments to the salvation package. "Yes, you're saved by grace," they say, "but you must always maintain your salvation by not going to dances or movies, not playing cards, etc." No. Now, as then, you're saved by God's grace not your own works.

## ACTS 16–17
### Refusing to Complain

— • —

Paul and Silas had been falsely accused, illegally beaten, and thrown in prison. They could have loudly complained and threatened legal action. Instead they sang songs worshipping God. Their Christian attitude, choosing joy over bitterness, allowed God to perform a great miracle. Far too often complaints and murmurs short-circuit the power of God. Remember the Israelites wandering in the desert? They complained because they doubted God loved them. They thought He was against them. Never doubt God's love no matter what your circumstances.

## ACTS 18–19
### Tested Promises

---

When Paul was in Corinth, the Lord promised He wouldn't permit anyone to attack and harm him. But after a while, the Jews of Corinth made a major attack against Paul (Acts 18:9–12). What happened to God's promise? Well, it proved true. Enemies attacked but couldn't harm Paul. God will often give you promises as well, and He may allow His promises to be tested. But stand firm; remind the Lord that He gave you specific promises and you're counting on Him coming through for you—and they won't fail.

## Wolves among Sheep

Paul warned the pastors of Ephesus that eventually wolves in sheep's clothing would sneak in and seize unsuspecting sheep. Even some leaders would distort the truth, seeking to have their own followers. So Paul warned faithful pastors to be on guard (Acts 20:29–31). You too must watch out, because many false teachers seek to pervert true doctrine. If you hear a strange teaching from a charming speaker, beware lest you be deceived. Tell your concerns to responsible Christians whom you respect or to church leaders, and have them check the person out.

.................................................................................................

.................................................................................................

.................................................................................................

.................................................................................................

.................................................................................................

.................................................................................................

.................................................................................................

.................................................................................................

.................................................................................................

.................................................................................................

## Rights of Citizenship

When the commander of the Roman garrison ordered Paul to be tied up and whipped, Paul informed him that he was a Roman citizen. It was a serious violation to beat a citizen. As a citizen of this country, you too have inalienable rights and shouldn't hesitate to insist on them. Romans 13 states that the police exist to punish evildoers, and it's not being vindictive to enjoy the protection of the law. Remember, however, that there are times when it's God's will for you to relinquish certain rights in order to bless others.

## Ways God Rescues

When the Roman commander learned that forty armed men wanted to murder Paul, he ordered two hundred soldiers, seventy horsemen, and two hundred spearmen to take Paul to Caesarea by night (Acts 23:12–24). The last time Paul faced a similar threat, a couple unarmed men had lowered him over the city wall in a basket (9:23–25). God isn't limited by a set way of doing things whether defending you, bringing finances, restoring relationships, etc. He is perfectly capable of working outside the box. Don't limit Him by insisting that He do things a certain way.

## ACTS 25–26
## True and Reasonable Faith

As Paul was explaining the Christian faith to the Roman governor, Festus, the governor protested that all this was just too much to believe. Paul responded that he wasn't making it up. He assured Festus that what he was saying was not only true but was reasonable as well. It made logical sense. Your faith is based on solid historical evidence, and the events of the New Testament describe what actually happened in known geographical locations in real time. Knowing this, you can love God with your heart and soul *and* with your mind (Matthew 22:37).

## ACTS 27–28
### *Purpose behind Disasters*

Paul was aboard a ship sailing to Rome when a fierce storm swept them along day after day for two weeks. The passengers gave up hope, but in the end they shipwrecked on Malta. They had lost all their belongings, but the good result was that many Maltese became Christians. Your world may be upside down now, and tragedy may have left you confused and despairing. But God is able to get good out of bad situations (Romans 8:28). Trust that He's at work in even the unfortunate circumstances of your life.

# ROMANS

❧―❦―❧

Some call Romans a "theology textbook" for its thorough explanation of the Christian life. Paul begins by describing God's righteous anger against sin (Romans 1–2), noting that everyone falls short (3:23). God provides the only way to overcome sin: by you receiving the righteousness of God (3:22). Being justified (made right) through faith in Jesus, you consider yourself to be dead to sin. God's Spirit gives life (8:11) to all who believe in Jesus and calls you to present your body as a living sacrifice (12:1). With God's help, you can overcome evil with good (12:21).

## ROMANS 1–2
### God's Glorious Creation

———•◦•———

When you watch the waves crashing on a stormy seashore, or sit and take in a beautiful sunset, or observe nature on a walk through the forest, you get a sense of awe of the divine. You get an inkling of the Creator behind it all. You can begin to grasp, though not fully understand, God's invisible qualities—His magnificent power and supernatural wisdom (Romans 1:19–20). As David said, the heavens proclaim the glory of God; all nature declares that it's the work of His hands (Psalm 19:1). Take time to observe God's creation today.

## ROMANS 3–5
### Righteousness through Faith

In Romans, Paul explains that you're not saved by your own good deeds and efforts to be righteous. Forget striving to impress God. Rather, you partake of the righteousness of God Himself when you put your faith in Jesus Christ, when His Spirit enters your heart. You're justified freely by His grace (Romans 3:22–24; Galatians 4:6). You've been born again through faith in Jesus, so be sure to walk in that same Spirit, depending on God's love and grace, all the days of your life.

## Earning Wages, Receiving Gifts

Many people think they're good and moral and expect God to reward them (basically pay them wages) for their good deeds. They think they can earn eternal life in heaven. But all people are sinners, and the wages they actually earn is death, separation from God. But in stark contrast to earning wages, God offers mankind eternal life as a *gift*. That means it's free. You don't have to earn it. You just have to open your hands and accept it. (See Romans 6:21–23.) Take time to praise God for His gracious gift.

## United with God's Spirit

You're born again if God's Holy Spirit dwells in your heart. But if anyone doesn't have the Spirit of Christ, they don't belong to Him because He places His Spirit in everyone who is His (Romans 8:9). Paul also states that whoever is united with the Lord is one with Him in spirit (1 Corinthians 6:17). Your spirit and God's Spirit dwell together in your body, and your union is much like a marriage. As you yield your life to Christ and ask Him to fill you with His Spirit, you become ever more one with Him.

## ROMANS 10–11
### Trusting God to Save You

Paul explained that when it comes to salvation, God makes no difference between Jew and Gentile. God is Lord of all and richly blesses all who call on Him. Everyone who calls on the name of the Lord will be saved (Romans 10:12–13). It's also good to remember this promise if you think you've sinned too greatly for God to save you. His promise still holds true: If you call on the name of Jesus, you'll be saved. If you've walked away from Him, He still can save you. So call out to Him today.

# ROMANS 12–14
## Christian Duties

Romans 12:9–21 contains the teachings of Christ in a nutshell. Love others sincerely. Hate evil. Hold tightly to good. Be devoted to one another in love. Honor one another. Be patient when suffering affliction. Pray faithfully. Share with fellow Christians in need. Be hospitable. Bless those who persecute you. Don't curse others. Rejoice with those who rejoice. Mourn with those who mourn. Live in harmony with one another. Don't be proud or conceited. Live at peace with everyone. Don't repay anyone evil for evil. Don't take revenge. Overcome evil with good.

## Focus on the Good

In Romans 16:19, Paul said that he wanted believers to be learned and knowledgeable about good things but innocent and even ignorant when it came to evil things. Some people will criticize you for sheltering your children (or yourself) from the bad influences of the world, but that's what you're supposed to do. You're to fill your mind with thoughts about things that are true, honest, just, pure, lovely, and of good report. If something is virtuous or praiseworthy, think on it (Philippians 4:8). For one thing, you'll have a lot more peaceful dreams at night.

# 1 CORINTHIANS

Paul founded the church in Corinth (Acts 18). While in Ephesus, he learns of serious problems in the Corinthian congregation and writes a long letter to address those issues. Paul urges them to be perfectly joined together (1 Corinthians 1:10). Paul commands them to cast wicked people out of the church (5:13), warning that the unrighteous shall not inherit the kingdom of God (6:9). The apostle also teaches on marriage, Christian liberty, the Lord's Supper, spiritual gifts, and the resurrection of the dead. In the famous thirteenth chapter of 1 Corinthians, Paul describes the ultimate virtue, love (see 12:31).

# 1 CORINTHIANS 1–3
## The Wisdom of God

The Lord made the entire world and all that is in it by His great wisdom. Just taking one look at the amazing complexity of the DNA helix should convince you that God is unfathomably wiser and more intelligent than you are. The amount of coding that exists to make life function is mind-boggling. And it's the same with God's plans. For example, a crucified Messiah may look illogical and weak at first glance, but it's a breathtakingly powerful plan (1 Corinthians 1:22–25). Think you're wise? The wisdom of this world is foolishness in God's sight (3:19).

---

In the Feast of Unleavened Bread, the Jews were to rid their homes of all leaven (yeast) and leavened bread. Even a little yeast can multiply greatly until there's so much of it that it can leaven a huge batch of dough. So Paul said for you to get rid of the old yeast and live your life not with the old bread leavened with malice and wickedness but with the unleavened bread of sincerity and truth (1 Corinthians 5:6–8). Jesus said that the leaven of the Pharisees was hypocrisy (Luke 12:1). Avoid that too.

## Love Builds You Up

---

It's good to have knowledge. Proverbs repeatedly states that godly knowledge, understanding, and wisdom are to be desired. But there are limits to the value of human knowledge. Just knowing facts and figures and being able to quote them rapid-fire will puff you up with pride. Whereas if you have love in what you say, it builds you and others up. Knowledge puffs you up while love edifies you. A little knowledge can be dangerous, so the Bible warns that if you think you know something, you don't yet know as you *ought* to know (1 Corinthians 8:1–2).

.................................................................................

.................................................................................

.................................................................................

.................................................................................

.................................................................................

.................................................................................

.................................................................................

.................................................................................

.................................................................................

.................................................................................

## Running the Race

Paul frequently compared the Christian life to running a race. He pointed out that though all the runners run, only one gets the prize. So he urged you to run in such a way as to get the prize. That means not only finishing strong but staying within the lines (rules for life). Paul also observed that those who competed in Olympic games underwent strict training. They did it for a mere laurel wreath, but you do it to get an eternal crown (1 Corinthians 9:24–25). So be thankful if God is strict with you. It shows He's training you.

## Part of the Body

---

The church is the body of Christ, and each individual Christian is a particular part. God has put the body together so that it can work as a whole, all of its parts contributing something and every part having an invested interest in the well-being of the other parts. Think of it: If one part suffers, every other part knows about its pain. If one part is honored, the entire body rejoices with it (1 Corinthians 12:24–27). This is the ideal. . .and it should also be the reality. How true is this of you and your church?

........................................................................................

........................................................................................

........................................................................................

........................................................................................

........................................................................................

........................................................................................

........................................................................................

........................................................................................

........................................................................................

........................................................................................

## Importance of the Resurrection

Gnosticism taught that only spiritual things were good, and the entire visible, physical world was evil. So some Greeks argued that they wouldn't come back to life in "evil" physical bodies. But remember, Jesus lived on earth in a physical body, and His body was raised from the dead. In fact, His resurrection saves you (Romans 10:9). If Christ *hadn't* been raised, your faith would be useless (1 Corinthians 15:12–14). Dan Brown and other modern writers have made Gnostic heresies popular again, but you are to reject them (1 John 4:3).

# 1 CORINTHIANS 15:20–58;
# 1 CORINTHIANS 16
## Shining Like Stars

------·•·------

God has a wonderful future planned for you! He has promised to raise your physical body back to life, transforming it into a glorious, eternal body that glows with the beauty and splendor of God. It will be raised imperishable, shine with glory, and be full of tremendous power. Daniel 12:3 promises that obedient Christians shall shine like the stars forever. But remember, some stars glitter with more splendor than other stars. So live for Christ wholeheartedly now so that *more* of God's glory might rest on you (1 Corinthians 15:41–44).

# 2 CORINTHIANS

Corinthian believers have addressed some of the problems Paul's first letter mentions, though there are still those who question his authority. He is forced to declare hardships he's faced serving Jesus, describing how he has worked harder, been beaten more, been thrown in prison more than other believers (2 Corinthians 11:23). Paul also suffers from a "thorn in the flesh" (12:7), which God refuses to take away, telling him that His strength is made perfect in weakness (12:9). Paul's parting warning is for the Corinthians to examine themselves, whether they are truly in Christ, walking as He walked (13:5).

## 2 CORINTHIANS 1–3
### God's Strength

---

Paul experienced many troubles in Ephesus (see Acts 19). He was under great pressure, far beyond his ability to endure, so that he despaired of life itself. He wrote that God allowed this to teach him not to rely on himself but on God (2 Corinthians 1:8–10). Have you ever experienced such intense trouble or pressure that you almost gave up? How did God strengthen you and help you survive it? Are you going through such a time now? Cry out to God. He promised that He would help you (see also 4:7–10).

# 2 CORINTHIANS 4–7
## Wasting Away

Do you sometimes feel like your physical body is wasting away either because of advancing age or prolonged illness? The apostle Paul knew how that felt, but he gave cause to hope! Though your *body* is fading, God is strengthening your *spirit* day by day (2 Corinthians 4:16–18). You may say, "But the weaker my body becomes, the more discouraged my spirit gets." Don't lose heart. It can hurt when you exercise; your muscles literally tear in order to be rebuilt stronger. Draw close to the Lord and your aching spirit will grow stronger.

## 2 CORINTHIANS 8–10
### Reaping Rewards

———•✦•———

Under the Law of Moses, God's people were required to tithe, to give 10 percent of their income to God. In this dispensation of grace, believers are to give what they have decided in their hearts to give. If you choose to give 10 percent, good for you! But whatever amount you give, don't give it because you feel under pressure to do so. God loves people who give cheerfully. Also remember, if you sow just a few seeds, you'll reap a small harvest. If you sow generously, you'll reap a great harvest (2 Corinthians 9:6–7).

# 2 CORINTHIANS 11–13
## Strength in Weakness

Can you say, like Paul, that you *delight* in weaknesses, in insults, in hardships, and in persecutions (2 Corinthians 12:10)? Probably not. Why could Paul say that he did? Because Jesus had told him from the get-go that He'd use him to accomplish great things *if* he was willing to suffer greatly (Acts 9:15–16). With that in mind, Paul embraced his troubles and finished running his race (Acts 20:23–24), knowing that the weaker and more incapable he was, the more Christ's power rested on him. You too must learn that when you're weak then you're strong.

# GALATIANS

Writing to several regional churches, Paul marvels (Galatians 1:6) that many Galatian Christians have turned from their freedom in Jesus back to the rules of Old Testament Judaism. Some Jewish Christians tried to compel Christians to live as the Jews did (2:14)—to be circumcised and keep the endless Law of Moses—to be saved. Even the apostle Peter was swayed by this error and compromised with it (2:11–13). But Paul argues strongly that no man is justified by the law in the sight of God but that the just shall live by faith (3:11).

## GALATIANS 1–3
### Saved by God's Spirit

Paul asked the Galatians if, after *beginning* (being saved) by the power of the Spirit, were they trying to *finish* (mature in Christ) through their own efforts (Galatians 3:3). You may wonder how they could've been so foolish, but Christians today frequently slip into such a mind-set. They know they were saved by grace but think it's now up to them to *keep* themselves saved through good works or to mature and produce fruits of the Spirit. Continue to walk in His grace. Only Christ can keep you and mature you. (See also Galatians 5:4, 22–23.)

## GALATIANS 4–6
### Faith Expressed in Love

———•◦•———

Paul said in Galatians 5:6 that the only thing that counts is faith expressing itself through love. Often people know you're a Christian only if they see evidence of it in your life. There's a close relationship between faith and love. To begin with, you must have faith that Jesus loves you and has the power to save you. Then, after He saves you, you feel love for Him (see 1 John 4:19). And since He commands you to love your fellow man, you're then motivated by His love to reach out to others (Galatians 5:14).

# EPHESIANS

—❦—

Paul had started the church in Ephesus (Acts 19) and now explains in detail the church members' relationship to Jesus Christ: you are part of His body on earth; He is the head (Ephesians 4:15). So it is advantageous for you, as an individual body part, to grow up into Him in all things. Through Jesus, God has reconciled both Jews and Gentiles to Himself (2:11–18). This new life should result in pure, honest living in the Church and in the home (chapters 4–6). Paul also describes the armor of the Spirit in Ephesians 6.

# EPHESIANS 1–3
## Knowing God Better

—•◦•—

Paul's prayer for first-century believers in Ephesians 1:16–19 also applies to you. Paul prayed that God would strengthen you with power through His Spirit and that you, being rooted and established in love, would be able to grasp how vast and profound is Christ's love for you. He prayed that you might become fully aware of this love that surpasses knowledge and that you might be filled with all the fullness of God. Pray this prayer for yourself and others. It may be quite different from most prayers you pray, but give it a try.

..................................................................................................

..................................................................................................

..................................................................................................

..................................................................................................

..................................................................................................

..................................................................................................

..................................................................................................

..................................................................................................

..................................................................................................

..................................................................................................

## EPHESIANS 4–6
### Children of Light

---

In a stiff sermon spanning Ephesians 4 and 5, Paul warned that you must walk in your new life in Christ and have nothing further to do with greed or sexual immorality, since those caught up in such sins have no inheritance in the kingdom of Christ. Paul said not to let anyone deceive you into thinking that you can give yourself over to such sins and still know Christ. Seek to do what pleases the Lord (Ephesians 5:3–10). It's often difficult to deny yourself, but God can breathe His strength into your spirit.

........................................................................................................

........................................................................................................

........................................................................................................

........................................................................................................

........................................................................................................

........................................................................................................

........................................................................................................

........................................................................................................

........................................................................................................

........................................................................................................

# PHILIPPIANS

With sixteen references to "joy" and "rejoicing,"
Philippians is the apostle Paul's most upbeat epistle,
even though he wrote it while a prisoner in chains
(Philippians 1:13). Paul thanks the church at Philippi
for its financial support of his ministry (1:5) and
encourages its people to always rejoice in the Lord
(4:4). He assures them that he—and therefore they
and you—can do all things through the power of the
Spirit who strengthens him (4:13). Paul admonishes
Christians to live worthy of the glorious Gospel and
to expect persecution for Christ's sake (1:27–30).

## Don't Grumble

You read in Philippians 2:14 that you're to do everything without grumbling, but while that's easy to say, it can be very difficult to practice. You may have a tendency to complain when things go badly. What then is the solution? Paul says to rejoice in the Lord always. You may think, "Not only am I *not* to complain, but I should put on a happy face? That's difficult!" It may be, but it's proven to work. In every situation, however stressful, pray with thanksgiving. Determine to be consistently happy and grateful, and eventually you will be.

## Losing All to Gain Christ

———•◦•———

You know from reading the Gospels that you're to hold material things with a loose grip, always willing to release them. The same goes for dreams and accomplishments and possessions. Whatever you once considered great gain should hold little allure for you now. Instead, you are to be steadfastly determined to know Christ. Paul said he considered all things garbage compared to Christ. You don't have trouble letting go of *garbage*, do you (Philippians 3:7–8)? Remind yourself of that next time God requires you to surrender something.

# COLOSSIANS

False teaching by smooth-talking, persuasive individuals (Colossians 2:4) had infiltrated the church at Colosse, apparently causing some people to add unnecessary and unhelpful elements to their Christian faith. Paul sent a letter to the Christians there to remind them of the superiority of Jesus over Jewish rules and regulations (2:16), angels (2:18), and anything else. Jesus is the image of the invisible God, the firstborn of all creatures that exist (1:15). The entire nature of the Godhead dwells bodily in Christ (2:9). And His divine, all-powerful Spirit now dwells inside you!

## COLOSSIANS 1; COLOSSIANS 2:1–15
### The Deity of Christ

In his letter to the Colossians, Paul gives a powerful description of the divine nature of Christ. He writes that the Son is the image of the invisible God. When you love Jesus, you're loving the eternal God, His Father. All things have been created *through* Jesus and *for* Him. What is more, He holds all Creation together by His power (Colossians 1:14–17). This should impress upon you the importance of obeying Jesus' teachings. After all, He wasn't simply some carpenter-turned-Messiah. He was and is almighty God.

## Focus on Spiritual Things

---

As you live your life day after day, you're constantly impressed with the solidity and the importance—even the urgency—of physical things. You need shelter, so you must work hard to pay your mortgage or rent. You need a vehicle, clothing, and groceries, so you must work hard to earn money for them. But all this sometimes means that you risk being swallowed up by physical things. So God reminds you to set your heart on things above, to focus on eternal rewards not on fleeting earthly things (Colossians 3:1–2).

# 1 THESSALONIANS

In this letter to another church he had founded (see Acts 17), Thessalonica in northern Greece, Paul teaches on the second coming of Christ, which is an issue of great concern to many of the Thessalonians. They are suffering frequent persecution, so they pray that Jesus will return soon and deliver them. Paul describes how Jesus will return but doesn't say exactly when. The important thing, in his words, is that believers walk worthy of God, who has called them into His glorious kingdom (1 Thessalonians 2:12). Walking worthy also includes being pure and avoiding sexual immorality (4:3–8).

# 1 THESSALONIANS 1–5
## Lead a Quiet Life

It seems that everywhere Paul went in the book of Acts, foes shouted threats, enemies plotted his death, and riots broke out. So it might seem surprising that Paul tells you to make it your ambition to lead a *quiet* life, to mind your own business and work hard so that you may win the respect of outsiders (1 Thessalonians 4:11–12). Furthermore, he tells you to pray for your rulers, that they will *let* you live a peaceful and quiet life (1 Timothy 2:1–2). You don't need to constantly have trouble to prove you're obeying God.

# 2 THESSALONIANS

Shortly after writing 1 Thessalonians, Paul dictates a second epistle. Apparently, a letter claiming to be from Paul had left the Thessalonians shaken and troubled (2 Thessalonians 2:2) at the thought that Jesus had already returned and left them behind. Paul assures them that the event is still in the future. A number of Thessalonian Christians, anticipating Jesus' imminent return, have quit their jobs and are wandering around agitating fellow believers. Paul commands them to get back to work and stop mooching off others. If they refuse to be gainfully employed, hardworking believers shouldn't feed them (3:10).

## 2 THESSALONIANS 1–3
### God Will Protect You

———⋅◦⋅———

In 2 Thessalonians 1:5–7, Paul comforted the Christians of Thessalonica who were being persecuted and told them that Jesus would one day judge their persecutors. But for now, persecution was to be expected. Jesus promised that people will persecute you if you follow Him (John 15:18–20). Paul went so far as to promise that anyone who lives a godly life will suffer persecution (2 Timothy 3:12). But it's important to remember that the Bible also promises that the Lord will strengthen you and protect you from the evil one.

# 1 TIMOTHY

The first of three "pastoral epistles," written originally to church leaders about pastoring their flocks, 1 Timothy contains the aging apostle Paul's insights for a new generation of church leaders. Timothy had often worked alongside Paul but was now pastoring in Ephesus (1 Timothy 1:3). Paul warns him against legalism and false teaching (chapter 1), lists the qualifications for pastors and deacons (chapter 3), and describes the behavior of a good minister of Jesus Christ (4:6) in the final three chapters. Paul also devotes quite a bit of space to giving instructions on the care of widows.

### Love and Sincere Faith

Demonstrating Christian love in your daily life springs from a sincere faith in Jesus Christ. Paul explained that love comes from a pure heart, a good conscience, and a sincere faith and that those who leave these often turn to meaningless talk. Instead of genuinely caring for others and loving people, they end up in pointless arguments (1 Timothy 1:5–6). You must hold on to faith and a good conscience. Those who reject these shipwreck their faith (v. 19). Having a sincere faith and a good conscience are vital to staying on track for Christ.

# 1 TIMOTHY 4:9–16; 1 TIMOTHY 5–6
## Beware the Love of Money

---

In 1 Timothy 6:5–10, Paul warned that Christians who get caught up in materialism or who seek worldly wealth wander from the faith. This is why Jesus said to be on your guard against greed, because true life doesn't consist in an abundance of possessions (Luke 12:15). It's certainly no sin to be wealthy, but guard against finding your security and happiness in wealth. Put your trust in God instead. Let Him be your chief joy. You can prove that you don't trust in money by being generous in your giving (1 Timothy 6:17–19).

# 2 TIMOTHY

*※◀━━━◀※◀※*

Second Timothy is the last letter of Paul. Addressed to Timothy, his beloved son in the faith (2 Timothy 1:2), the book warns the young pastor against false teaching and urges him to live a life of purity. Timothy should expect trouble because all who will live godly lives shall suffer persecution (3:12), but God will be faithful. Paul affirms that the Lord will deliver him from every evil scheme and preserve him and usher him into His heavenly kingdom (4:18). Paul begs Timothy to join him quickly, as the time of his death is near at hand (4:6).

## 2 TIMOTHY 1–4
### Play by the Rules

———— •◦• ————

Second Timothy 2:5 states that if you compete as an athlete, you won't receive the prize unless you compete according to the rules. You've probably heard of athletes who ran fast but out of bounds and received no award or who used performance-enhancing drugs and were stripped of a medal. It's the same for Christians: God longs to reward you greatly for your lifetime of service, but if your actions don't stand up to scrutiny, they'll be burned. You yourself will be saved, but you'll suffer from their loss (1 Corinthians 3:10–15).

.................................................................................

.................................................................................

.................................................................................

.................................................................................

.................................................................................

.................................................................................

.................................................................................

.................................................................................

.................................................................................

.................................................................................

.................................................................................

# TITUS

Paul had left Titus on the Mediterranean island of
Crete to appoint elders, set leaders in place, and
organize the fledgling church (Titus 1:5). Known
for their laziness and questionable behavior, the
believers of Crete need the kind of church leader
who holds fast to the faithful Word that he has been
taught, so that by using sound doctrine, he can exhort
and convince argumentative people (1:9). Paul also
urges everyone who calls themselves a Christian to
be submissive to rulers and authorities (3:1) and
to devote themselves to doing good works (3:8).

## Basic Salvation Reminders

Even in Titus, a letter about appointing church leaders, Paul reminds you that God saved you not because of righteous things you did but because of His mercy. He caused your spiritual rebirth through His Spirit and freely gave you eternal life (Titus 3:5–7). Have you ever wondered why Paul never stopped expounding on these most basic principles of salvation? It's because he knew that your strength, your joy—indeed, the very success of your Christian life—depend on you always remembering that God loves you deeply and saved you by His mercy.

*(Also read Philemon's devotional today.)*

# PHILEMON

Philemon is a "fellow laborer" (Philemon 1) of Paul's, and is a man who has refreshed other Christians with his love and generosity (7). But the apostle writes with a serious request—that Philemon forgive a runaway slave who apparently had stolen money from Philemon, fled Colosse, and ended up in Rome, where he met the apostle Paul and accepted Christ. Paul refers to Onesimus as his "son," one whom he had fathered while a prisoner in Rome (10). Paul urges Philemon to forgive Onesimus, to receive him as he would the apostle Paul, and to set him free (17).

## PHILEMON 1–25
### Motivated by Love

———————

Over the years, the apostle Paul had frankly commanded new Christians how to act once they became disciples of Christ. But when writing to Philemon, a mature Christian renowned for helping and giving (Philemon 5, 7), Paul was able to simply appeal to him to act out of love (vv. 8–9). Are you motivated by love? Do you need your pastor and your family and friends to constantly remind you about your duties and obligations as a disciple? Or are you sensitive to the Spirit, following the Lamb *wherever* He goes (Revelation 14:4)?

# HEBREWS

Written to Jewish Christians (hence the name "Hebrews"), this letter emphasizes the superiority of Christianity to Judaism. Jesus is so much better (Hebrews 1:4) than angels, Moses' Law, and animal sacrifices. For if the blood of bulls and of goats makes people pure, Hebrews asks, how much more shall the blood of Christ purge your conscience? (9:13–14). Jewish Christians, some of whom are apparently wavering in their commitment to Jesus, are reminded that Christ is the mediator of a better covenant that was established upon better promises (8:6)—a once-for-all sacrifice on the cross that provides eternal redemption (9:12).

## HEBREWS 1–3
### Avoid Drifting Away

The Bible tells you to pay careful attention to the teachings of Christ so that you don't drift away from Him (Hebrews 2:1). When you read His Word and hear Him speaking to you, don't harden your heart (3:7–8). Don't have a sinful or an unbelieving heart that turns away from God (v. 12). If you harbor unbelief, you'll slowly but surely pay less attention to Christ's words and eventually drift far from Him. If you have a sinful heart, you'll knowingly turn away from God. Avoid these by keeping your heart soft toward God!

## Jesus Empathizes

Hebrews 4:15–16 says Jesus empathizes with your weaknesses because He was tempted in every way like you are, but He didn't sin. This is why you can approach His throne confident that you'll receive mercy and find grace to help during crises. Often, precisely when you need God's mercy and grace the most, the enemy tries to convince you that you're not worthy of it, that the Lord is angry with you and won't hear you. If you're going through a dark night of the soul, take courage. God loves you, and the way to His throne is open.

### Jesus Saves You Completely

---

God declared that Jesus was a priest forever in the order of Melchizedek (Hebrews 7:17). The wonderful thing about Jesus living forever and having a permanent priesthood is that He's able to *completely* save you because He's always present to intercede before God for you. You can be confident that He who began a good work in you will perform it until the final day (Philippians 1:6). Don't ever worry that He's deserted you. He won't do that. He will never leave you or forsake you (Hebrews 13:5). His right hand upholds you (Psalm 63:8; Isaiah 41:10).

## A Strong Hope

Sometimes during long, dark nights, the Accuser will attempt to convince you that you're not even saved—though God can and does forgive all others, He can't forgive you. But rest assured that you've been redeemed. You can draw near to God with a sincere heart and with the full assurance that faith brings, certain that He has cleansed your guilty conscience. Hold unswervingly to the hope you have professed for years, knowing that He who promised to save you is faithful (Hebrews 10:22–23). God has forgiven you. Count it done.

## Have Faith in God

Anyone who comes to God in prayer seeking His help must believe that He exists. That's a no-brainer. Otherwise, why would you bother to pray? But here's a detail that often eludes people: you must also have faith that He loves you enough to answer you (Hebrews 11:6). This is the confidence you have when coming before Him in prayer: that if you ask anything according to His will, He hears you. And if you know that He hears you, whatever you ask, you know that you already have what you asked Him for (1 John 5:14–15).

## God Chastises His Children

Hebrews 12:5–8, 11 tells you not to be discouraged by the Lord's discipline and not to lose heart when He rebukes you, because the Lord disciplines those He loves. Think of hardship as discipline. And what children aren't disciplined by their father? They all are. It's God training you how to live as a Christian. He's aware that no discipline feels like tender love. It's painful. But if you patiently endure difficult times, you'll find that in the end, they produce a harvest of righteousness and peace for you. So hang in there!

# JAMES

⊰⊱

Paul taught that salvation is by faith alone and not by your own efforts (Romans 3:28), but James clarifies that good works will result if you have true faith. James asks what good is it if someone says he has faith in Christ but there's no evidence of any change in his life (James 2:14)? James encourages Christians to view hardships as opportunities for spiritual growth, to control your tongue, to make peace, to avoid favoritism, and to help the needy. If you are aware of good things you ought to do but don't do them, you sin (4:17).

## Continuing in the Word

James counsels you not just to listen to the Word but to do what it says. If you read the Word but don't obey it, you're only kidding yourself. But if you gaze intently into the law of Christ and continue meditating on it and living it, you'll be set free (James 1:22–25). Do you want to be Jesus' disciple? Then steadfastly hold to His teachings. You'll know the truth, and the truth will set you free (John 8:31–32). But remember, "knowing" the truth must be more than mere head knowledge.

## Submit to God, Resist the Devil

If you find yourself experiencing troubled thoughts that you can't seem to shake, you're likely under attack by the devil. How do you stop it? The first thing you must do is yield to God. That's because although pride creates a disconnect with God, His Spirit goes out to the humble. Let God be Lord of your life. If you sincerely seek Him and cry out to Him, He'll be present in your life with power. Then when you resist the devil, you'll have authority, and he'll flee from you (James 4:6–10).

# 1 PETER

As the early church grows, the Roman Empire begins persecuting Christians—and Peter assures believers that God is still in control. He warns them not to think the fiery troubles they go through are some strange thing. Rather, these are to test their faith. Hardships and temptations are no strangers to disciples of the Lord (1 Peter 4:12). What is the proper response to such suffering? Believers are to rejoice because they partake of Christ's sufferings. In the same way, when Christ returns in all His glory, they too will be filled with exceeding great joy (4:13).

# 1 PETER 1–2
## Enduring Fiery Trials

You may be experiencing unrelenting trouble and problems that leave you despairing and exhausted. You may wonder if God is still on your side. But most likely He is putting you through the fire. He's allowing your faith to be tested. It might not feel like it, but God is working good things in your life. He hasn't abandoned you to the enemy. He may allow you to be tested sorely, but He won't lose you. So rejoice! Endure the fiery test of your faith, and you'll receive glory and honor when Jesus returns (1 Peter 1:5–9).

# 1 PETER 3–5
## Give a Good Answer

—•◆•—

A verse in today's reading tells you to always be prepared to give an answer to any person who asks you why you believe in Jesus (1 Peter 3:15). People will ask you questions either because something you say strikes them as odd or because God has been working on their heart for some time. To give a logical reason, you have to know what the Bible says. So it pays to read it faithfully and pray before you read. Ask God to open your eyes and enable you to see great truths hidden in scripture (see Psalm 119:18).

# 2 PETER

In this epistle, believers learn that the Christian qualities of faith, virtue, knowledge, self-control, patience, godliness, and love (2 Peter 1:5–8), coupled with a reliance on scripture (1:19–21), will help them avoid the false teachings of those who cleverly slip in damnable heresies, even denying the Lord who bought them with His blood (2:1). Peter warns against licentious teachers who lead Christians into sexual immorality (2:17–19). Now aged, Peter describes the awe he felt those many years ago when he saw Jesus transfigured in glory on a mountaintop and heard God's audible voice (1:16–18).

## 2 PETER 1–3
### Assured of Your Salvation

———•◦•———

Second Peter 1:10–11 says to be careful to confirm that you're saved. That way, you'll never stumble and will receive a rich welcome into the kingdom of God. You know Jesus saves, yes, but do you find yourself questioning whether He has saved *you*? It might be because you're asking God to search your heart for sin, and when He shows you, you're faced with a sense of unworthiness. Of course you're unworthy! But it's God's love and grace that saves you. Remind yourself of verses like Isaiah 1:18; John 5:24; Acts 2:21; and 1 John 1:9.

# 1 JOHN

First John tackles a heresy that claimed Jesus had been on earth only in spirit not in body. John assures believers that everyone who denies that Jesus Christ came to earth in a physical body is inspired by an antichrist spirit (1 John 4:3). John wrote that he knew Jesus personally, had looked upon Him, and had touched Him (1:1). Knowing these facts leads to a saving belief in Jesus. Saving belief leads to obedience; but even when you sin, you know that God is faithful and certain to forgive you your sins when you confess them (1:9).

## Cleansed from All Sin

---•◦•---

If you've been a Christian for some years and are trying your best to please God, He will probably keep you on a short leash. He will convict you quickly when you sin against Him or others. If you do sin, immediately repent. God has promised to forgive you. If you walk in the light as He does, you'll have fellowship with Him, and the blood of His Son, Jesus, will cleanse you from all sin. Know this: if you confess your sins, He will forgive you and cleanse you from them all (1 John 1:7, 9).

## 1 JOHN 3:10–24; 1 JOHN 4–5
### God Is Love

The statement "God is love" is a basic truth. Believing it and understanding it will affect your entire concept of God, reveal what He expects of you, and permeate your whole attitude, filling you with love for Him. In 1 John 4:7–8, you're told to love others because such love comes from God. If you genuinely love others, and care for them the way you care for yourself, it's proof you've been born of God's Spirit and know Him. But if you fail to love others, it shows that you don't know God like you should.

# 2 JOHN

Addressed to "the lady chosen by God and to her children" (2 John 1 NIV), either a family or a church, 2 John disputes the heresy that Jesus hadn't been physically present on earth. The letter is a reaction to the Gnostics, who taught that Jesus was spirit only and had merely *appeared* to die on the cross. The Gnostics taught that people's bodies—indeed, the entire physical world—are evil, having been created by a lesser deity. John insisted that this teaching came of the deceiver (7) and should be avoided—to the point of barring one's door against those who teach it (10).

## 2 JOHN 1–13
### Beware of Deceivers

You're commended to invite fellow believers into your home and offer them food, fellowship, and lodging (3 John 5–8). But beware! If someone perverts the Gospel of Christ, they have abandoned God, and you shouldn't invite them into your home (2 John 9–11). You'd just be helping them spread heresy. There are a number of so-called Christian sects that teach strange, unscriptural doctrines. Even people who attend mainline churches sometimes get tripped up into false doctrine. Avoid fellowship and Bible studies with them.
(*Read 2 John, 3 John, and Jude together.*)

# 3 JOHN

In this brief letter addressed to a believer named Gaius, 3 John praises those (like Gaius and another Christian named Demetrius) who lead in love as examples to the whole church (3 John 6). They are commended for showing kindness and hospitality to traveling evangelists. But 3 John also has harsh words for Christians like Diotrephes, who loves to have preeminence (9) and refuses to receive Christian ministers, even using his position as a church leader to excommunicate Christians who do show them hospitality.

# 3 JOHN 1–14
## Prospering in Every Way

The apostle John prayed that a fellow believer named Gaius would enjoy good health and that he would prosper financially just as his spiritual life was prospering (3 John 2). John wasn't espousing the "health and wealth" teaching that some modern Christians follow. But as a Christian, you're commanded to bless others. Since Gaius was *already* doing well spiritually—in the most important area of his life—John prayed for God to bless his health and finances as well. Pray for God to bless those you love in every way also.

# JUDE

---

Jude deals with the same problems Peter did in his second letter: false teachers who were leading the early church astray. Murmurers and complainers who walked according to their own lusts (Jude 16) were apparently using the grace and forgiveness of God as a cover for their sinful, lascivious lifestyles and were encouraging other believers to do the same. True Christians, Jude says, display God's love, show compassion, and work to pull out of sinful lifestyles that lead to destruction (23). Jude gives a graphic description of punishment in the afterlife to warn believers away from heresy.

# JUDE 1–25
## Contend for the Faith

To contend means to struggle, and in a debate, it means to insist on or argue for something. This is what the Bible means when it urges you to contend for the faith that was *once and for all* entrusted to God's people (Jude 3). The Gospel was given to the church finished and complete. It doesn't need to be improved, watered down, or made more inclusive. So contend for the truth calmly but firmly. Don't argue. Believers shouldn't quarrel but must be gentle with everyone, able to patiently explain the truth to others (2 Timothy 2:24).

# REVELATION

Jesus Christ gives John a revelation of things that will soon come to pass (Revelation 1:1). First, He gives John messages for seven churches. Then the vision turns to the throne room of God, where a Lamb (5:6) breaks seven seals from a scroll, unleashing war, famine, and other disasters. A dragon and two beasts arise to demand worship. Angels pour out seven bowls of the wrath of God (16:1), and the upheaval destroys the evil world system. Afterward, Satan is thrown into the lake of fire (20:10). God then unveils a new heaven and a new earth (21:1).

## REVELATION 1–2
### Jesus in His Glory

———•◦•———

When you finally see Jesus, He will look far more wonderful than He did on earth. In His eternal state, His hair is pure white, His eyes blaze like fire, His feet are like glowing bronze, His voice sounds like rushing waters, and His face shines like the sun (Revelation 1:14–16). The wonderful news for you is that when you see Him in heaven, *you* will be radiant like Him (1 John 3:2), albeit to a lesser degree. Jesus promised that when His kingdom comes, you too will glow like the sun (Matthew 13:43).

........................................................................................

........................................................................................

........................................................................................

........................................................................................

........................................................................................

........................................................................................

........................................................................................

........................................................................................

........................................................................................

........................................................................................

# REVELATION 3–5
## Promises to Overcomers

Life for Jesus can be very difficult at times, so it's important to encourage yourself by reading the promises He makes to those who put their faith in Him, who overcome the trials and tests of this life (see Revelation 3:5, 12, 21). Jesus originally made these promises to the seven churches of Asia Minor, but they hold true for all Christians of all time. For example, if you overcome, Jesus has promised to never remove your name from the Book of Life (3:5). So how do you overcome? Simple. Believe in Jesus (see 1 John 5:5).

## REVELATION 6–8
### No Sorrow in Heaven

---

Some of the most beautiful promises in the Bible are found in Revelation 7:15–17. There, the Bible promises that you who have suffered for Jesus' name, gone hungry rather than deny Him, and endured unrelenting tests, trials, and afflictions will stand before the throne of God, where you'll be bathed in the glorious light of God's presence. Jesus Himself will be with you and guide you to streams of living water, and your heavenly Father will personally wipe away every tear from your eyes. In that day, you will know for certain that it has been worth it all.

# REVELATION 9–11
## The Seventh Trumpet

———•◆•———

Revelation 11:15 says that when the seventh angel sounds on his trumpet, a multitude of voices in heaven will shout that the kingdoms of the earth have become the kingdom of God and His Son and that Jesus will now reign forever and ever. In the day that Jesus returns, He will bring His rewards with Him and will mightily recompense you for every bit of good you've done, for every sacrifice you've made, and for every generous and loving deed you've done (v. 18). Nothing will be forgotten (22:12). The Lord will make good on this promise.

## REVELATION 12–14
### Overcoming During Evil Days

———— ◆ ————

When you read these chapters about the rise of the Antichrist, the mark of the beast, and the worldwide persecution of Christians, you may wonder how you'll survive such times. But Revelation 12:11 declares that you'll triumph over the evil one by the blood of the Lamb, shed to forgive your sins and to shield you from wrath. You'll overcome evil by holding fast to your faith and by refusing to be cowed even when it might cost your life. It will take courage to face such days, but Jesus will be with you.

## The Armies of Heaven

Many people ask why, if God is a God of justice, He doesn't judge and punish the wicked. Yet when He actually *does* judge, people then ask why He's so hard and doesn't show mercy. They question God's motives and methods no matter what He does. Revelation 16:5–7 declares that in earth's final days, God will send such powerful plagues upon the earth to punish the wicked that He needs to remind believers that He is just in all these judgments. You too do well to be convinced that God's judgments are true and righteous.

# REVELATION 18–19; REVELATION 20:1–6
## When Jesus Wages War

Some people wonder how a gentle Jesus could thunder down from heaven to wage war on the wicked (Revelation 19:11–14). But Paul wrote persecuted Christians many years previously that one day Jesus would be revealed in blazing fire to punish the wicked (2 Thessalonians 1:7–9). It's important to know that the Good Shepherd who lovingly seeks you out when you've gone astray and gently bears you on His shoulders also takes up His staff in fierce anger to fight off the wolves that attack you. These are all manifestations of His love for you.

## Heaven on Earth

In Revelation 22:3, God reassures you that one day He will no longer seem to be absent or distant but will dwell openly on earth among His people, and that includes you. You will rejoice eternally in the fact that you're His son or daughter and that He Himself is with you and is your God. In that day, He will remove all sorrow from you. You will live forever in His presence and never again experience mourning or crying or pain. That kind of wonderful future is well worth waiting for.

## ABOUT THE AUTHOR

**Ed Strauss** was a freelance writer living in British Columbia, Canada, who passed into heaven in 2018. He authored or coauthored more than fifty books for children, tweens, and adults. Ed had a passion for biblical apologetics and besides writing for Barbour, was published by Zondervan, Tyndale, Moody, and Focus on the Family. Ed has three children: Sharon, Daniel, and Michelle Strauss.

LIKE THE 5-MINUTE BIBLE STUDY?
TRY OUR 5-MINUTE PRAYER PLANS!

## *The 5-Minute Prayer Plan for Women &
The 5-Minute Prayer Plan for Men*

Many Christians yearn for a dynamic prayer life, but we
often get stuck in a repetitive routine of prayer. These
practical and inspirational guides will give you new ways
to approach prayer with 90 focused, 5-minute plans
for your daily quiet time. These prayer plans explore
a variety of life themes appropriate for all ages.

Women - Paperback / 978-1-68322-831-8 / $5.99
Men - Paperback / 978-1-68322-832-5 / $5.99